I was impressed with the ... eousness. I encourage oth... mation throughout God's ... Geoffrey Higham for many years, and he is a true Christian brother to us.

—Pastor John Andy
Assemblies of God, Cardwell
Queensland, Australia

Geoffrey Higham and his wife, Margaret, are beloved and faithful members of our congregation where Geoffrey serves us in his gift of a teacher. I believe with all my heart that his book is inspired by the Holy Spirit. I consider that it is new wine sent to revive and strengthen the end-time church.

As his pastor and longtime friend, it is my pleasure to endorse both the man and this challenging teaching.

—Pastor Joe Strumia
Innisfail Home Church
Queensland, Australia

I found this book to be very readable yet profound. The Holy Spirit seems to be talking directly to the reader.

Written with a faith-filled simplicity that I have personally observed has led the author through life for the past twenty-two years.

A walk in the Spirit—guided by one walking in the Spirit for twenty-seven years.

An intimate look at the work of the Holy Spirit in a faith-filled person's life.

An alternative book title could well be *Taking the Holy Spirit Seriously by One Who Has Done So for Twenty-Seven Years*.

This book is an invitation to take what the Holy Spirit says concerning righteousness seriously, at face value. This invitation is issued in a readable style using a language that reflects the deep faith and trust of the author in the day-by-day guidance of the Holy Spirit. This walking in the Spirit life is also seen in his wife and all of their seven adult children who are serving in various churches throughout Australia and Europe.

—Francis Crane
Former Administrator, Saint Monica's Cathedral
Cairns Diocese, Australia

Reading this book, you will meet a man and his wife whose inner convictions of the righteousness of the Lord Jesus Christ and holiness unto the Lord called for total obedience to the Word of God, the exercising of the faith of God in adversity and implicit trust in God who delivers positive direction to every promise given to mankind.

Geoffrey and Margaret have been very good friends of mine for many years. Geoff is an architect in his own right and has always been keenly interested in the real plan of God for His church throughout the world.

As you read, you will be challenged and motivated to walk closer to Jesus. I believe that you will be inspired to develop a deeper trust in the Word of God and to walk uprightly in total obedience to every instruction for life given directly from the throne room of God the Father.

Geoffrey and Margaret have allowed the Holy Spirit to guide, guard, and govern their Christian journey for the greater part of their lives, and you will, undoubtedly, want to develop a greater hunger for such a lifestyle as you absorb the events graphically articulated throughout this book.

This book is simply an extension of the level of trust, obedience, and delight in the only true God of heaven and earth as two such people have experienced the best of their love for Him.

—Bernie Gray
International Director
Full Gospel Businessmen's Fellowship International

Geoffrey Higham begins his book with the shattering news from his doctor that he, as a young man of forty-eight years, had only a few months to live. The reality of the situation became very clear. He had to come into a right relationship with God. Jesus Christ came for that purpose, and so he unfolds his own journey of faith and knowing who he is in Christ.

To say, "I am righteous," is to some a form of pride, but according to the Bible, and as this book makes very clear, it is our standing with God in Christ.

Geoffrey Higham and his wife, Margaret, came across our path many years ago, and through that contact, I was able to be the vehicle or umbrella under which they could serve the Lord for six years in Kagoshima in south Japan.

Many stories could be told of their trials and triumphs in those days, but always they were reaching out to people—never afraid to pray for people who were in need.

There are many testimonies, some of which are in this book of remarkable answers to prayer—like the lady in Ireland who unbeknown to them was carrying in her womb a dead child. Sensing she had a need, they prayed the prayer of faith, without the knowledge of the real situation, and the child in her womb came alive again, and was born normally.

God is so good, and this is illustrated throughout the book, but it also shows us our responsibility as believers to believe the Word and act on it and live a righteous life before the world.

Geoffrey lays a good foundation and then goes on to deeper things of the Holy Spirit, which is where every believer should follow. My prayer is that all who read this book will learn to walk the righteous walk and enter into the glory of God.

—Reverend Lionel H. Thomson
Founder and President, Japan Good News Ministries
Pastor Emeritus, Christian Life Centre
Niiza City, Saitama Ken, Japan

I recommend this book as a guide to a true Christian life. Geoffrey Higham is a well-known and respected Christian in the northern parts of Queensland. Although not of my denomination, we have been friends in Christ for over twenty years. His book comes as no surprise to me. It will be published at a time when the church of our Lord needs redirection and, I believe, a return to the righteousness of the days of the first apostles.

—Reverend Jack Wood
Priest of the Diocese of Brisbane
Anglican Church of Australia

Go and Sin No More is a wonderful insight into a true gentleman, Geoff Higham. Geoff has lived a very interesting life and takes you for a journey into that life with this book. While taking that journey, you will also capture an insight into his life and his God, backing up comments with scripture.

Geoff has travelled many bumpy and dusty roads and now shares these experiences. He has always represented himself as a thorough gentleman in our community and someone I have considered as an elder.

He has gone through many phases in his Christian walk and now has the maturity and knowledge to reflect on his journey.

I know this book will enthuse and encourage many people, and I hope it will help those people walk more closely with God.

—C. R. Barry D. Moyle
Mayor
Innisfail, Queensland, Australia

Go and Sin No More

Geoffrey Higham

CREATION HOUSE PRESS
A STRANG COMPANY

Go and Sin No More by Geoffrey Higham
Published by Creation House Press
A part of Strang Communications Company
600 Rinehart Road
Lake Mary, Florida 32746
www.creationhouse.com

This book or parts thereof may not be reproduced in any form, stored in a retrieval system, or transmitted in any form by any means—electronic, mechanical, photocopy, recording, or otherwise—without prior written permission of the publisher, except as provided by United States of America copyright law.

Unless otherwise noted, all Scripture quotations are the author's paraphrase.

Scripture quotations marked KJV are from the King James Version of the Bible.

Cover design by Terry Clifton

Copyright © 2004 by Geoffrey Higham
All rights reserved

Library of Congress Catalog Card Number: 2003111488
International Standard Book Number: 1-59185-409-1

04 05 06 07 — 8 7 6 5 4 3 2 1
Printed in the United States of America

Acknowledgments

My deepest appreciation to:

The Spirit of Jesus Christ who has patiently and graciously taught and tested me over the twenty-seven years leading up to the publishing of this book. Thank You, Father.

My wife who stands beside me in fair weather and in foul; whom I love very much and who encouraged and endured me during the days of writing this book. Thank you, my darling.

The following faithful friends and exhorters without whose support I may have given up.

Gary Smith, Dan and Ann Quaid, G. B. Higham, John and Marg Rowell, and Joe Hall. May God bless you—I know He will; for we each reap what we sow.

My mother.

Miyako Hirano.

Allen Quain, Virginia Maxwell and all the staff, including the telephone operators, at Creation House for their kindness, diligence, and advice during the publication process.

My Referees, Bernie Gray, Joe Strumia, Francis Crane, Barry Moyle, Lionel Thomson, Jack Wood, John Andy, and Raynold Bori. Thank you for believing the message which God has placed in my heart.

All of the precious people of my generation who at various times and in different places have been a part of my life. We passed like ships in the night, but you are a part of me, and this book.

And our seven children and their spouses, our fifteen grandchildren and two great grandchildren who are all close to my heart. Thank you for standing with me.

Contents

Foreword xi
Introduction xv
Chapter 1   A Month to Live 1
Chapter 2   The Word of Righteousness 8
Chapter 3   Walking Squeaky Clean 17
Chapter 4   Decoy in China 20
Chapter 5   Centipedes and the Law 23
Chapter 6   In Step or Out? 27
Chapter 7   Saved From What? 32
Chapter 8   Rio and Righteousness 37
Chapter 9   Toronto or My Dignity? 40
Chapter 10 Friend—Stay Healed 45
Chapter 11 Professor Cho and Overcoming Sin 50
Chapter 12 Atom Bomb and Cannot Sin 53
Chapter 13 Beat Every Temptation 57
Chapter 14 A Big Toe and Balance 66
Chapter 15 Reformation Now 73
Chapter 16 A Close Friend 78
Chapter 17 Faith Through Love to Heaven 81
Chapter 18 Lifestyles of Holiness 85
Chapter 19 Dreams, Visions, Deserts, and H. W. Connie 89
Chapter 20 Doing Is Righteousness 94
Chapter 21 A Miracle in Ireland and Faith Has Works . . . 98
Chapter 22 A Tiny Flock 104
Chapter 23 The Beautiful Lady 109

Foreword

Geoffrey A. Higham teaches and preaches God's word boldly and simply, with the power of the Holy Spirit, and with an enthusiasm that captures the heart of the reader. He has learned that God's righteousness of a sin-free life can be effective in every walk of life and that it will work for anyone who will believe it and apply it according to God's word. His uncompromising message in *Go and Sin No More* and his teaching and preaching stir up and motivate the hearts of today's born again Christians in the body of Christ to live a holy life before God.

This is a man with a timely word for the church today. The impact of this message on God's righteousness, I believe, is going to shake the nations of the earth and bring further revival and reformation to the body of Christ.

What a refreshing book! Straightforward, sound in doctrine, and full of insight from God's Word. It is obvious from Scripture that now is the time that we must make a concerted effort to blow the whistle and halt the great falling away that is taking place in the West before our eyes. Even the media of this world are lamenting the sad and sinful condition of the church. The kingdom of God is righteousness, peace, and joy in the Holy Ghost. (See Romans 14:17.)

Nothing excites me more than the truth of God's Word, and this book is certainly filled with that. This is not just Geoffrey Higham's opinion. It is what the Word of God says; when you are born of God, you go and sin no more. We must live in the lifestyle of God's kingdom. If you know the truth, the truth will set you free! Glory!

Geoffrey A. Higham is an ordained pastor of Christian Mission Centre International. I would recommend this book to all pastors, church leaders, and born again Christians who have a great heart to serve the Lord on this earth.

—Raynold Bori, C.M.C.
National and International President
Director of Bethel Bible College
Senior Pastor of Global Harvest Centre
Republic of Vanuatu, South West Pacific

A Message From the Author

In August of 2002 the Holy Spirit spoke to my heart, "My people are hungering for righteousness. Therefore, write down all that I have been teaching you. See to it that it is published as a book so that it will reach my people throughout the earth." He said, "You are one of God's End-Time sons who are called to walk and teach in the Spirit of Elijah, preparing the way for Christ's return. And blessed are those who hunger and thirst after righteousness for they shall be filled and they shall be His spotless bride."

On the book's completion, He spoke to me again in the early hours of the morning, "Tell my church that the pleasures of sinning will destroy my people in this world and in the next for all eternity. I have created you for pleasures, but if you seek first any pleasure beside me, you will never have peace, happiness, or contentment. Once I become your abiding pleasure, I will provide other pleasures for you to enjoy, and these pleasures that flow from Me will add to the righteousness, peace, and joy which are in Christ Jesus. Delight yourself therefore in Me, and I will grant to you pleasures that your heart desires. Make me your exceeding great joy. And all these things will be added to you."

Introduction

That we being delivered out of the hand of our enemy, sin, should serve Him without fear, in holiness and righteousness all the days of our life (Luke 1:74–75, author's paraphrase).

The message in this book is not about your past lifestyle. It is not about how to cope with sinning. It will show you God's way of being finished with it forever.

This book is not a theoretical treatise about sin. For years I was bound by it. The biggest obstacle that I faced was not knowing the source of my spiritual cancer.

Over a period of time, God exposed the source of my iniquities. He thereby set me free.

I invite you, dear reader, by absorbing this book in the spirit of a little child, to join me in this freedom and so secure your inheritance of eternal life.

Can it be an accident that this book is in your hands? I do not believe so!

I invite you with all of my heart to join me in a prayer as you begin your adventure.

> *Dear Jesus, take my heart, Lord, fill it with one accord with yours. Take it, shake it, break it, and remake it until it is one with yours.*
>
> *Please expose my old and stubborn mind-sets. Open my eyes afresh to the truth of your Son's words and promises. Show me if there is deception in my foundations. May this be the start of a new day of a lifestyle without sin. I want to stand before you blameless through your power and my faith. I acknowledge that it will all be in your grace. May I truly be freed to serve you for what you have called me to be. Draw me closer to You by your love. I want to be a worthy ambassador of our Royal King Jesus and to see you forever in your kingdom. Amen.*

Chapter 1

A Month to Live

To Him who is able to keep us from falling and to present us faultless—be glory and majesty, dominion and power now and forever.
—Jude 24–25

It came as a terrible shock to me as my doctor turned and said: "You have only a few months to live." I was forty-eight years old, and forty-two of those years were spent as a Christian. The doctor's words tore something from my face—the mask I had worn all of my adult life. Instantly I knew that my faith, which I had presumed to be great faith, had all along been a deception of my own wishful thinking. Glued to my seat in the doctor's office, I saw a sinner with head bowed, standing before a righteous judge.

He had given His life to set me free. I knew it, yet I had failed Him. I would not be able to look Him in the eye.

> You Lord render to each of us according to our ways for you alone know the hearts of each one.
> —I Kings 8:39

Driving back home slowly along the wet roads I felt scared. My life as a Christian had been a sham. Every Sunday in church they said I was saved. But saved from what? Since being *saved*, I had continued sinning—just not so openly.

My face was like a mask, and behind its smile I found it easy and comforting to accept the plausible theory that the saints, being human, are also sinners. They said that God understands and accepts us that way. They had Scriptures to support their ideas.

After that visit to the doctor, things had changed. I was being called into His presence. In my gut I knew that God, for all His loving kindness and mercy, cannot be mocked.

> For God will bring every work to be judged, every secret thing we do, whether good or bad.
> —ECCLESIASTES 12:14

It was not death that I feared. It was my judge, Jesus Christ my Lord.

I had mocked Him throughout my life with a "sin–repent, sin–repent" syndrome. The scenario, repeated weekly at the city's courthouse, was about to become a reality for me in God's holy court.

Outside the earthly court room the defendants laugh, smile, and joke. But once inside, while standing alone before their judge, they become strangely downcast, pale, nervous, and tongue-tied. Courtroom reality always comes as a shock to the accused.

I thank God that by His grace, I still had enough conscience left to know that our God does not accept hypocrites. I knew it would be useless to try the old excuse: "I admit that I have sinned but I am only human." I would not be judged on my humanity, but on my sins.

> If our heart condemns us, God is greater than our heart and knows all things. Only when our heart does not condemn us can we have confidence towards God.
> —1 JOHN 3:20–21

I felt dirty. The good that I wanted to do, I did not. The sinning I did not want to do, I had done. I had lived my entire so-called Christian life this way. I felt angry and frustrated.

In desperation I began praying for a way out that would set me free from sinning before I died. I understood all too well that the wages of sin is eternal death.

In answer to my prayers, God sent me a new friend, Mick Mullins. He saw my need and with quiet assurance said: "Geoff, you need the baptism of the Holy Spirit." (See Acts 1:5.)

I thought him a bit weird, but took his advice. Beside my bed every night I would pray, inviting the Holy Spirit to come into me and baptize me. Our Lord Jesus waited six long months, and took me to the edge before He filled me with the Holy Spirit.

I remember it vividly—it was midnight, and I was kneeling by my bed. He came through with wave after wave of indescribable *love*. In the end it was too overwhelming, too wonderful, and too powerful—I had to plead with Him to tone it down.

On that night that I will never forget, *He gave me my personal Pentecost*. I was immersed in the *river of life*. At that instant I became a new person. Physically I was healed of my life long disease of asthma, as well as my more recent health ailment—hardening of the arteries. Both diseases were once to be the cause of my imminent death.

Spiritually, I was a new creation, experiencing His personal love for me in a very real way. Here was my chance for a new life.

Medical science had dismissed me as incurable and dying. It was His Spirit alone that healed me and restored me to perfect health. Since then, He has given me twenty-seven more years of health, vigor, and of being in love with Him.

> The Holy Spirit sheds God's love abroad in our hearts.
> —Romans 5:5

My doctor had given me about another six months to live, but my Jesus had other plans. That *wonderful* night as I lay immersed in His love, I knew that God had given me a *second chance*. Because of my ignorance, I was forgiven. I could almost smell the fattened calf on the spit.

> But I obtained mercy, because I did it ignorantly in unbelief. And the grace of our Lord was exceedingly abundant with faith and love, which is in Christ Jesus.
> —1 Timothy 1:13–14, kjv

Over the next few months, I had the new experience of losing all desire for the pleasures of sin. The *spirit of Jesus Christ had turned me into an overcomer*. His love flowed through me in waves. I had no alternative other than to love my neighbor.

> If we know that He is righteous, then we must know that everyone who *does* righteousness is born of God.
> —1 John 2:29

Sadly, but in God's plan, my pastor sat me down and told me that my honeymoon experience would soon be over. I would then return to earth and return to sinning like other Christians, including pastors.

The seed of doubt was sown. Soon it produced its fruit of sin; I was horrified. But glory be to God, by His grace I determined to search the Scriptures for myself. I had been given a taste of His glory.

Surely I was meant to live in it, in Him, for the rest of my life. In the footsteps of Paul the apostle I began my search by groping in the dark. I had never before searched out anything in the Bible. I had thought it wise to trust in others who were accepted teachers to show me the way.

It took me twenty-seven years to sort out the scriptural truth of what the Holy Spirit started to do in me on that most wonderful night of my life.

One night twelve years into this learning period, the Holy Spirit audibly spoke to me. He simply said three words, "Go to Kyushu." He did not say why. So after discovering in my Atlas that Kyushu is one of the main islands of Japan, I packed my bags and left my business in the hands of my son-in-law, Lance Dodds. A month later my wife and I boarded a plane for Tokyo. There were many tears shed at the airport as we left Cairns for we have a large family of seven children and at that stage there were ten grandchildren. Praise the Lord the airline Qantas upgraded us from economy seats to first class. He sent us off in style! While in Japan with my dear wife, I was isolated from my familiar world and set apart with Him—*the Spirit of truth*. He kept me there for six years.

My search revealed what the New Testament describes as the *word of righteousness*. (See Hebrews 5:13.) It is a doctrine that is in one sense the very core of the entire Bible from Genesis to Revelation. It is found in Jesus Christ. It is not a new doctrine, but I believe it is His time to restore it to the Church. *There is a sense of urgency even that fits these perilous shoals through which the church is passing.*

> If any man will do His will, he shall know of the doctrine, whether it be of God, or whether I speak of myself.
>
> —JOHN 7:17, KJV

According to what has taken place in my own life and some of my friends' lives, I believe that rediscovering the Doctrine of Righteousness will bring God's people into a twenty-first century Reformation. The great worldwide outpouring of the Holy Spirit during the twentieth century has prepared the way for it.

The Doctrine of Righteousness is about how to secure our house against the thief, sin. It is not about how to deal with that thief if he gets inside. It is about how to bolt the door and how to keep it bolted. It is about turning your house into an impregnable fortress. Make no mistake, that thief will not give up trying to gain entry for he was once a guest in your house.

The Doctrine of Righteousness is more easily taught (caught) than defined, but I define it in the words of the apostle Paul, for it was from his New Testament writings that I discovered the doctrine. He writes to us: I thank God that you were once the slaves of sin but now, having obeyed the doctrine which was delivered to you, and having been made free from sin, your old slave master, you now have become slaves of righteousness (author's paraphrase; see Romans 6:17–18). Please note that he uses the past tense because his new disciples in Rome have been, without question, obedient to his teaching which has set them free from sinning. It is the teaching that he gives in chapters six through eight. In chapter eight he summarizes the Doctrine of Righteousness this way: "There is therefore now no condemnation to them which are in Christ Jesus, who walk not after the flesh, but after the Spirit. For the law of the Spirit of life in Christ Jesus hath made me free from the law of sin and death" (Rom. 8:1–2, KJV). Once again please notice that he uses the past tense even though he is writing to the relatively new believers in Rome. Paul is adamant that believers who are walking in the Spirit have been set free from the previously unavoidable control of sin. Paul explains the doctrine to the Galatian church this way: "I am crucified with Christ: nevertheless I live; yet not I, but Christ liveth in me: and the life which I now live in the flesh I live by the faith of [in] the Son of God, who loved me, and gave himself for me" (Gal. 2:20, KJV). Paul is here identifying himself as a normal believer who is walking by faith. He could just as easily have written "we spirit-led believers" in place of the pronoun "I."

To the Ephesian church of relatively new believers, he speaks of the doctrine this way: put on the new man of God who after God has been created in righteousness and true holiness. Yes, the Doctrine of Righteousness is about accepting by faith the promise of Christ that every baptized believer who is walking in the Spirit has become a new creation. (See Ephesians 4:24.) Apostle John states that this new creation who is born of God cannot now continue sinning. (See 1 John 3:9.) It is the doctrine of which Jesus Christ prophetically spoke when he said that anyone who commits sin is a slave of sin, but he whom the Son sets free (from sinning) is free indeed. (See John 8:34, 36.) We cannot walk in the doctrine by sight (understanding), so do not attempt to.

You, dear reader, can see that the Doctrine of Righteousness which I am going to teach to you in this book is plainly nothing but scriptural truth from the Bible.

I respectfully suggest that down through the years the church (generally) has lost the doctrine because it is impossible to understand, and *it is a faith walk from start to finish.* Once we lost it there was no way that any but a few could be seen to be walking in it, and that is another contributing factor to its loss. I will, however, prove to you from Scripture that it is crucial for obtaining our future eternal inheritance. Shall we pray this prayer with our lips:

> *Dear Holy Spirit, in the name of Jesus, I beg you to kindly clear my mind of any old mind-sets that I cling to and are*

not of you. Please impart to my mind the truths in the scriptures which I am going to read in this book. I am not going to look back on my past failures, but I am thirsting for more of the new wine. Thank You, Lord, that I am going to learn how to keep the door shut and bolted. Amen.

I the Lord have called thee in righteousness.
—Isaiah 42:6, kjv

I am the Lord: that is my name: and my glory will I not give to another.
—Isaiah 42:8, kjv

Chapter 2

The Word of Righteousness

This I pray…that ye may be sincere and without offence till the day of Christ; being filled with the fruits of righteousness, which are by Jesus Christ.
—Philippians 1:9–11, kjv

Our rented home in Japan overlooked the wide, deep, and picturesque harbor beside the city of Kagoshima. On the opposite shore to the city stands the lazily smoking volcano known as *Sakura Jim*a, which in English means *Cherry Blossom Island.*

Frequently volcanic ash spurts out of that beautiful, towering mountain, and when the city is in the path of the wind the ash falls softly as a snowfall. Up to 25 millimeters (one inch) of fine black sandy ash can cover the streets and houses in one night.

They gave it the name *Sakura* because the original inhabitants likened the descending ash to the gently falling delicate pink and white petals of the Japanese cherry blossoms in spring. However, this was positive thinking. The ash that came up out of the bowels of hell and forced us to tightly shut our windows to keep out the black sand could never be compared with the beauty of standing under a Japanese cherry tree while blossoms blow in the spring breeze against the backdrop of a clear blue sky.

My words cannot describe the days in early April in Japan when all 120 million people spend a day of celebrating on blue tarps under the cherry blossoms planted in groves throughout the nation. They form a gorgeous peaceful canopy where *ottosan* (dad) and his family spend the day eating, drinking, singing, and dancing. It is not often that the Japanese miss *shigot*o (work) and relax together, but work stops on Sakura festival day and the wine flows.

It was mid-August. We had just finished our lunch of raw fish and the traditional *moogie cha*, a cool refreshing drink made from roasted barley. Lying on the floor of our bedroom, since most Japanese use the floor as the bed, I closed my eyes and asked the Lord: *please give me just one place where I can preach the gospel where it will not fall on deaf ears and concrete-encased hearts.*

It must have been the appointed time for within a few seconds I received a vision, as bright as any television screen, of the large bow of a black hulled cargo ship. In the vision I was standing on a wharf looking up at it for quite some time, but nothing was happening. Then, the scene was withdrawn suddenly.

As I went out the front door on that hot August day, I called to my wife, Margaret: "I am going to drive around the docks for an hour or so." My little red Nissan took me down the hot narrow roads to the port area where there were often ten or so ships tied up at the wharves. I was glad I could visit the cooler area by the sea—I needed some relief from the incredibly hot, breathless, and humid days, which permeate the country from the end of June till the start of September.

After driving around the port area for about an hour, I had not yet seen a black ship. I was about to give up when, at the berth nearest my home, I came across the only black hulled ship in the harbor. It was tied to the public wharf.

In obedience to the dream, I parked the car and walked over to look at the black bow of the 20,000-ton cargo ship. There I heard voices somewhere up on the decks. I waited for some fifteen minutes and at last a man's face appeared over the gunwale. I caught his eye and called out, "hello, there." I learned that they had been forced into the port of Kagoshima because of a seriously ill crewman. The captain of the ship had already taken the sick man to a hospital in our city, and the doctors had told him that the man was not expected to live. Because Filipinos speak English fluently but know little Japanese, the captain had been praying that the Lord would send him an English-speaking minister of the Christian religion. He was visibly startled and a little emotional when I entered his cabin and introduced myself as a Christian missionary. Within the hour, the captain had assembled in the large galley the ship's crew. With my guitar I was able to lead them for an hour of praise, worship, and praying for the dying man and for peace to the crew. I was rewarded by seeing the peace on their faces as they watched me go down the gangplank. Praise to the Lord for I was at that time the only missionary in the whole city of one million people in Kagoshima City.

This visit was the beginning of my ministry to the ships, which brought cargo to our harbor from all over the world. Often our upper room in Hirakawa would be filled with Koreans, Nigerians, Greeks, Fijians, or Filipinos. I discovered that these ship captains and their crews were hungry for fellowship and prayer. Many gave their hearts to Jesus for the first time. Once again the Lord started it all with a vision. It was opportune that English is the second language for most races in the world.

God knows our every need. When hearts are crying out to Him, He is never slow to answer with a shower of blessings.

The apostle Paul uses the term *word of righteousness* in his letter to the Jewish Christians in Hebrews 5:13. As Jews, they knew without question that the whole purpose of God's law was to keep them righteous in order to be eternally saved on judgment day. Through their knowledge of God's laws of good and evil, they would have known they were all unrighteous sinners.

Like everyone who lived before Christ, they were short of the requirements of God's glory. Paul wrote to remind them that only since the coming of Messiah Jesus has a lifestyle of righteousness become an attainable reality.

The Bible teaches us that God created mankind righteous and in friendship with the Creator. Being sinless, mankind possessed eternal spiritual life. God warned Adam not to partake of a certain type of knowledge. Man's knowledge of God's law of right and wrong.

God forewarned Adam that this knowledge of good and evil would cost Adam his eternal life. Sadly, envious Satan deceived

Adam's wife into believing that God loved them too much to punish them with death. She chose to believe Satan rather than God, and obtained the knowledge of God's law.

Adam foolishly followed his wife. They both lost their righteousness and came under the power of sin. It was earth's *greatest disaster*. From that point on, all of Adam's descendants until the end of time were to be born under the power of a *slavemaster* called sin.

> For ye were the slaves of sin.
> —Romans 6:20

But God can use valleys to turn shepherds into kings.

> The desire of the righteous shall be granted.
> —Proverbs 10:24, kjv

Four millennia later, the unwritten *law of the spirit of life in Christ* was given to restore the descendants of Adam to righteousness. Once again God gave His people the privilege of being able to walk as righteously as Adam and his wife. (See Romans 8:1–2, 4.)

> The Lord loveth the righteous.
> —Psalm 146:8, kjv

The Doctrine of Righteousness is not for kindergarten Christians. Paul wrote to Jewish converts that they must leave behind the elementary doctrines. (See Hebrews 6:1–3.)

I believe that now is the time to do so. Dear reader, are you willing to join me? I believe most of you are. Please join me and we will sit together and feast on the finest food in the pantry of the Word of God.

As we begin to get comfortable, let us recall the next disaster to strike mankind. God destroyed the face of the earth by flood. It came because of mans' unrighteousness.

And the Lord said to Noah: "Enter the ark, you and all your household; for you alone I have seen to be righteous before Me in this time" (Gen. 7:1, nas).

God saved Noah and his family because Noah lived righteously and hated sin. Noah's salvation is the example for all generations that the *righteous lifestyle guarantees eternal salvation.* We obtain it by exchanging our own life with Christ's life. We possess it in faith.

> The unrighteous shall not inherit the kingdom of God.
> —1 CORINTHIANS 6:9, KJV

Paul writes to us that the reason we will not be condemned on judgment day is if we have walked free from sinning through faith in His promise that "the law of the Spirit of life in Christ Jesus hath made me free from the law of sin…" (Rom. 8:2).[1]

But they are overcomers who walk by faith in His promises.

> The law of the spirit of life in Christ Jesus has set me free from the law of sin…
> —ROMANS 8:1–2

> The righteous shall give thanks to Your name and dwell in Your presence.
> —PSALM 140:13

What exactly is righteousness? We find the answer in the Word of God. The renowned prophet Ezekiel clearly defines righteousness in three separate chapters of his writings in the Bible. (See Ezekiel 3, 18, and 33.) Inspired by the Holy Spirit he writes:

> When a righteous man doth turn from his righteousness, and commit iniquity, and I lay a stumbling block before him, he shall die: because thou hast not given him warning, he shall die in his sin, and his righteousness which he hath done shall not be remembered: but his blood will I require at thine hand. Nevertheless if thou warn the righteous man, that *the righteous sin not*, and he doth not sin, he shall surely live, because he is warned; also thou hast delivered thy soul.
> —EZEKIEL 3:20–21, KJV, EMPHASIS ADDED

Therefore we see that righteousness means to be without sin. Man comes up with other definitions, but I prefer God's. Throughout this book I use the word *righteous* to mean *without sin*. Personally, I found Ezekiel 3:20–21 to be worth memorizing. Righteousness, we will find, is the lifestyle we must lead in order to be assured of our future inheritance in the *eternal kingdom of Jesus Christ*.

> The righteous shall inherit the land, and dwell therein forever.
> —Psalm 37:29, kjv

It is obvious that unless we have stopped sinning we cannot carry the name righteous. Man has introduced the theory that a saint can also be a sinner. John rejected that theory two thousand years ago. In his first New Testament letter he writes to us:

> Let no man deceive you: he that doeth righteousness is righteous.
> —1 John 3:7, kjv

It should be obvious that until we have stopped sinning we cannot carry the name *righteous*. How can a saint be a sinner? Can black be white? Can hot be cold or lukewarm? Can north be south? Can the door be both shut and open? John pulled the rug out from under us two thousand years ago. I repeat that he wrote: "Let no man deceive you: he that doeth righteousness is righteous" (1 John 3:7). He also says, "All unrighteousness is sin" (1 John 5:17). I believe that we cannot avoid the use of sensitive issues in the cause of our Lord Jesus and His life of victory.

> Any person who commits sin is of the devil.
> —1 John 3:8

Righteousness, therefore, is a personal action. John looks to put an end to the theory that says sins committed after conversion are hidden from God's sight by the righteousness of Christ.

As Christians we are required by God to walk in the grace of Christ's righteous life living through us. Paul reminds us of this when he writes:

> It is no longer I who lives but Christ who lives in me.
> —Galatians 2:20

John confirms it by writing:

> If we know that He is righteous then we must know that everyone who does righteously is born of Him.
> —1 John 2:29

We do not lead a righteous lifestyle by striving. We lead a righteous lifestyle by our ongoing faith in Jesus Christ and His promises. By obeying the Holy Spirit who lives within us, we walk in Christ's righteous life. This is the sole reason for a Christian to continuously celebrate and give thanks.

A sinner who celebrates in God's presence in a church meeting is therefore deluded or pretending. Our beloved Messiah Jesus teaches:

> Whoever committeth sin is the servant of sin…If the Son therefore shall make you free, ye shall be free indeed.
> —John 8:34, 36, kjv

When Jesus spoke those words, the devil must have been thunderstruck. He knows that God always fulfils His promises. I believe we should be thunderstruck too—I know I am. Sadly, it appears that the church will have to get a direct hit by one of His lightning bolts before it will shout to the world: "He has set us free from sinning."

One reason that the Jews of today find it hard to understand that Jesus is their promised Messiah is they know the Bible promises that the Messiah sets people *free from sinning*. Christians often fail to make this claim. I believe we fail because we walk more by sight than by faith in this area of being set free from the power of sin.

As a Jew, John was simply being biblical when he wrote:

> For this purpose, the Son of God was manifested so that He would destroy the works of the devil, Whoever is

born of God does not, and cannot, commit sin.
>—1 John 3:8–9

The Bible is emphatic that the unrighteous shall not inherit the kingdom of God. Our lifestyle therefore, after having been reconciled to God through Christ's blood, needs to be one of ongoing day-by-day righteous living.

> Anyone who abides in Him does not sin.
>—1 John 3:6

Therefore I believe that "being born of God" must carry on as a daily state of abiding in Him by faith.

> And without righteousness [holiness] no person can see God.
>—Hebrews 12:14

The psalmist concludes with:
The mouth of the righteous speaks wisdom. The law of God is in his heart. The Lord will not condemn him at the judgment. (See Psalm 37:30–31, 33.)

---

[1] Of course I agree that it is possible to stop walking by faith in the promises of Christ and so fall into sinning, but my teaching strictly follows the scriptural pattern that Paul uses in Romans. At this point of his letter he does not want to talk about sins which can be forgiven. No! He is strongly insisting Christ has already set us free from the law of sin which previously controlled us (see Romans 7:23) and that this is the reason why we will not be condemned with sinners at the judgment. I am convinced that the step-by-step revelation in the letter to the Romans is exactly as the Holy Spirit wants it. From experience I also know that failing to believe Paul's forthright statement that we have been absolutely, indeed, set free from sinning cracks open the door that leads to sin. Paul and I consider that we would be dishonoring our Lord Jesus if we did not stand shoulder to shoulder with Him on His promise that He Himself sets us free from sinning. (See again John 8:34–36.) If we are not

wholly committed to the truth that we are dead to sin and alive to God in Christ Jesus, we will never accept the Doctrine of Righteousness. What confidence would we have in an airline which issued parachutes to its passengers? Yes, we all know that it is possible for planes to crash, so why are there no parachutes? I will leave you to work that one out. That is right—the Doctrine of Righteousness is all about successful victory; it is not about possible defeats. It is the way that the Holy Spirit teaches, the way Paul teaches and the way I teach it. I would be failing Christ and His Body if I do not keep insisting over and over that a faith walk in the Spirit keeps us free from sinning. It is the very reason why John can write that anyone born of God cannot sin (not cannot continue sinning while they are in the state of being born again of God). I am not concerned about wearing the label Christian; I am concerned about bringing all believers into walking in the Spirit by faith, for in that way they are always fulfilling God's will. (See Romans 8:4.) I am teaching how to drive the car, not how to repair breakdowns. I am teaching grasshoppers that now they have become giants. Other writers are more than competent to teach us about how to handle a crash. In fact, if you go into any church doctrine you will find it overloaded with how to handle a mishap both scripturally and unscripturally. Is this not the reason that our western society, starting with the church, has reached possibly an all-time low in morality? The cracked open door has swung wide open, and the church appears to be holding it open. Why is part of the church ordaining homosexual ministers? Have we gone mad?

Chapter 3

Walking Squeaky Clean

The name of the Lord is a strong tower: the righteous run into it and are saved.
—Proverbs 18:10

Many mothers in Japan give their toddlers tiny slippers that squeak with every step. It delights the round-faced juniors and tells *o ka san, mummy,* where they are. Whenever I heard the squeak, squeak, squeak, I would think *if we do not walk in the promises of God, they cannot squeak for us.*

The promises of God, like little slippers, are lifeless if we do not walk in them. The squeaking mechanism is hidden inside the heels of the slippers. The promises of God are hidden inside the pages of the Bible.

First we must set aside time to search for God's promises. Then, by *faith* we must walk in them. Just one step in faith brings them to life. Try it—you'll like it.

> The kingdom of God is in righteousness, peace and joy is in the Holy Spirit.
> —Romans 14:17

The great apostle Paul writes to us:

If, when we were enemies of God, (by our sins) we were reconciled to Him by the death of His Son, then how much more having been reconciled, shall we be *saved by His life?* (See Romans 5:10.)

It is certainly worth celebrating—His life working through us is going to save us from God's wrath at the judgment. He confirms this in his letter to the Galatians church when he writes:

> Our righteousness comes by exchanging our own life

> for Christ's life—by faith. For it is no longer I that lives but Christ who lives in me.
> —GALATIANS 2:20

I take that promise, step out in faith in it, and walk *squeaky* clean each day. I am elated that Christ has taken care of my past life, by His death, and my future by his life working through me. Paul writes that we are to leave behind the kindergarten doctrines that reconciled us to God. (See Hebrews 6:1.) They brought us to the start of the race—now we have to run that race.

> Let us lay aside the sin that so easily besets us, and let us run the race before us with patience and perseverance.
> —HEBREWS 12:1

Because it is Christ's life, and not our own, we are free from further sinning, for Jesus cannot sin. No sin means no condemnation. At the end of the race my crown awaits me. I receive it for having run righteously—in Him.

I have finished the course—henceforth there is laid up a crown of righteousness which the Lord who judges righteously will give me on that day (author's paraphrase; see 2 Timothy 4:7–8).

You may have been taught that your own righteousness is as filthy rags to God. This, of course, is true—that is the righteousness, which comes from the law of commandments. (See Philippians 3:9.) But we walk in the righteousness imparted to us by the Holy Spirit, through faith in Christ Jesus our Lord. (See Romans 8:4.)

To whom much is given, much is required is a principle in God's kingdom. Therefore Christians will be the first to be judged. We will be held accountable for our actions from the day we were converted.

Spend your time here on earth in fear because our *Father judges us according to our works.* He does not judge us in regards to *who* we are; He holds us accountable for our works. So be *holy.* (See 1 Peter 1:16–17.)

Dear believer, there is no longer any reason for you to worry about your past mistakes. Jesus Christ has erased all of them. Even better, He is in charge of your future.

My young friend G. B. is leaving shortly for East Africa. He will be teaching in a missionary school. He is sending over his reliable Land Cruiser and a little furniture through a reputable shipping agent.

He is without worry because the shipping is guaranteed and fully insured from shore to shore. If we can trust man, how much easier it is to trust the written promises of God Almighty?

> For God has given us the guarantee of the *Spirit*.
> —2 Corinthians 5:5

> For as many as are led by the Spirit of God, they are the sons of God.
> —Romans 8:14, KJV

Each time I think of being His son I sing, shout, and dance around. If I lose my so-called dignity, so be it. Try it I'm sure you'll like it.

> My soul doth magnify the Lord, and my spirit has rejoiced in God my Saviour.
> —Luke 1:46–47, KJV

Chapter 4

Decoy in China

When I stepped off of the train that had carried me deep inside China, I felt relaxed and confident. My Chinese brothers in Christ told me that it was not illegal to take Bibles in my bags. I was in the pleasant company of a dozen Christian businessmen and their wives. Inside the station I stepped into one of the many queues leading to two stern-faced officials that wore red banded officer's caps and red armbands.

Beyond them I saw the X-ray machine that checked luggage. Beside the machine stood a group of grim-faced red hats. I began to lose my cool, and my hands started to sweat.

My visa was in order, so I successfully satisfied the first two men. I took my bags and strolled past the X-ray machine. Suddenly the place exploded with high-pitched shouts and screams. It was the grim faced brigade.

They snatched my bags away from me and emptied out my clothing and thirty Bibles. In a rude manner, they snatched from me my passport, and after leaving me to stew for an hour, they returned everything except the precious Bibles.

Later, in the hotel, my friends laughed and called me a "big Aussie *decoy duck*," for they had used the melee to slip past the machine undetected.

I, like you, do not want to face my final Judge with sweaty palms and a pounding heart. Thank God:

> Being justified freely by his grace through the redemption that is in Christ Jesus: Whom God hath set forth to be a propitiation through faith in his blood, to declare his righteousness for the remission of sins that are past, through the forbearance of God.
> —Romans 3:24–25, kjv

On our *new birthday* we were justified, and His righteousness was imputed to us. Our heavenly file received a tap from the delete key. But our name was not deleted from the Book of Life.

Until that day we had no righteousness before God. We all had *sinned and come short of God's requirements. In fact anyone who says that he had not been a sinner is a liar and makes God a liar.* (See 1 John 1:8–10; Romans 3:23.)

We started the salvation race completely righteous. Our baptism in the Holy Spirit empowers us to run that race righteously to victory. He is more than able to keep us from falling if we persevere in faith, working through love. (See Jude 24; Galatians 5:6.) Everyday we strive to exchange our life for His, coasting along in His promise that:

> We were crucified with Jesus nevertheless we live. But really it's not we who live, but Christ who lives in us. If the Law could achieve a life of righteousness then Christ would have died in vain.
> —Galatians 2:20–21

Whether or not we believe in *once saved always saved*, the Bible makes it certain that we must live a righteous lifestyle if we are to receive our eternal inheritance.

If we sin willfully after we have received the knowledge of the truth, there is no more sacrifice for sins. Instead, we are certain to face judgment and fiery indignation. (author's paraphrase; see Hebrews 10:26-27.)

Hudson Taylor toiled for twenty years as a missionary in inland China. Frustrated, he realized that they were teaching the Chinese a gospel that they themselves were not living.

In desperation, he went to search out the truth for himself. He finally discovered the promise of God in Galatians 2:20, which he called "the exchanged life."

From then on he was able to live what he taught. He asked the mission headquarters in London to only send people to the mission field that were filled with the Holy Spirit and were walking with Him.

For the righteousness of the law is fulfilled in us who walk according to the Spirit and not according to the flesh.

—ROMANS 8:4

Chapter 5

Centipedes and the Law

Commit your way to the Lord, trust Him—and He shall bring forth your righteousness as the light.
—Psalm 37:5–6

In Japan's farming communities, homes have a hole in the center of the living room floor that is about three feet deep and about two feet square. During the cold winter nights it is the mother's duty to place a tray of hot coals in the bottom of the hole before replacing the *kototsu* (square table with a heavy cloth skirt all round) over it and laying out the *o-hashi* (chop sticks). The family—already bathed and clean—comes to dinner in their bare feet. Each one lifts up the table skirt and sits down in their own place.

Their legs from the knees down hang warm and comfortable in the hole above the hot coals. The skirt covers their laps and stops the heat from escaping. It is a very pleasant experience from the waist down, but a heavy coat is needed to keep the torso warm.

Many winter nights our kind neighbors Seiichi and Ine Kusubae would invite us to sit around their kototsu to sip tea and talk, however broken our Japanese.

One memorable evening, a large centipede emerged from the hot pit and ran up on to my wife's arm. It was as long as my hand span and as thick as my little finger. She let out a scream and in flicking it off, it landed on me and ran up on to my head before I could flick it out the door.

We had many similar confrontations with the centipedes and snakes that live in the rice paddies of Nippon Land but never were we bitten. Many of the locals, however, suffered serious wounds, especially from the deadly *mamooshey adder*. The mamooshey is a short thick snake similar to our deaf adder whose bite can prove fatal. They lie still and wiggle the end of their tail to attract unwary birds.

One night after a farmer had gone to bed the deadly snake slithered into the bedroom and sunk its fangs into the farmer's big toe. We always stood firmly on the words of Scripture that promises immunity for believers walking in the Spirit. (See Mark 16:18; Luke 10:19.)

> Behold I give you power to tread on serpents and scorpions—and nothing shall hurt you.
> —LUKE 10:19

Getting back to the Doctrine of Righteousness, let us look at the Mosaic law. All of the apostles and most of the teachers of the early church were Jews. They had all tried to be righteous by memorizing and trying to obey the Ten Commandments and the rest of the laws. On the day of Pentecost, ten days after the Lord Jesus ascended into the heavens, the scales began to fall from their eyes.

For 1,500 years, the Jews had tried to establish their own righteousness by the Torah (law). Now their righteousness burst forth from within through the indwelling of the Spirit of God; they had been born again.

> For Christ is the end of the *law* for righteousness.
> —ROMANS 10:4, KJV

> And if righteousness could come by the *law* then Christ died in vain.
> —GALATIANS 2:21

It was not long before Saul, the great persecutor of Jewish Christians, literally had scales drop from His eyes. He was filled with the Holy Spirit and was led out into the desert. Saul was highly trained in the knowledge of the Torah but in the desert Jesus Christ taught him that while the *law* kills, the *Spirit* gives life. (See 2 Corinthians 3:6.) In Christ Jesus nothing avails but "*faith which worketh by love*" (Gal. 5:6).

We know that today many Christians still find it hard not to place some trust in the Ten Commandments or church laws in order to achieve righteousness. But God requires us to choose our master. He requires us to seek the righteous lifestyle of the unwritten law of the Spirit of life in Christ Jesus. (See Romans 8:2.) We are not to mix the new unwritten "law of the Spirit" with the written law of the Torah. We are in a *new covenant.*

Jesus expressed it this way:

> Neither do men put new wine into old wineskins; the skin would break, and the wine would run out and the wineskins would perish. Instead, they put new wine into new wineskins so that both are preserved.
> —MATTHEW 9:17

Paul learned the Gospel not from man but directly from the glorified Christ. He wrote chapter seven of his letter to the Christians in Rome to explain that as long as we remain under the Torah we are slaves to another unwritten law—the *law of sin.*

He reminds them that those under the *law of commandments* delight in the *law of God.* But, they find another *law* in themselves that makes war against God's *law.* They end up being captured by the *law of sin* against their will. (See Romans 7:22–23.)

He confirms it by writing: In our mind we were determined to obey the *law of God,* but with the flesh we obeyed the *law of sin.* (See Romans 7:25.)

The *law of sin* is more powerful than the human mind. If we are honest we will find this to be true through personal experience. However, the *law of sin* takes a person to *eternal* death. (See Romans 6:23; 7:24.) Paul also says the only way to stop sinning is by faith in the *law of the spirit of life in Christ Jesus.* (See Romans 7:25; 8:2.)

Israel, which followed after the *law of God* for righteousness, has not attained righteousness. But those who do not follow the *law* have attained it through the righteousness that comes by faith. (See Romans 9:31.)

Therefore it is obvious from New Testament Scripture that we cannot have a righteous lifestyle by attempting to follow the Ten

Commandments or any other parts of the Torah. If we find that our Christian walk turns out to be the lifestyle of sin that Paul describes in Romans 7, we can be sure that we have missed the boat.

Paul's writing faithfully describes the unrighteous lifestyle of a person who is still looking to the law of commandments for righteousness. He writes:

When we were in the flesh, the actions of sins, which were by the law, that worked in our own flesh and blood members to bring forth fruit unto death…But now Christians are delivered from the law that, being dead wherein we were held, we should now serve in newness of Spirit, and not in the oldness of the written (letter) law. (See Romans 7:5–6.)

In conclusion, Paul reminds us that Christians have died to the law and are set free from sinning. (See Romans 7:4; 8:2, 4.) So let us put on (by faith) the brand new man of God that is created in His righteousness and true holiness. I do—and it works. Try it—you'll like it. (See Ephesians 4:24.)

> Be found in Him, not having our own righteousness, which is by the *law*, but the righteousness, which is through faith in Christ.
> —PHILIPPIANS 3:9, *emphasis added*

Chapter 6

In Step or Out?

Sinners shall not stand in the congregation of the righteous for the Lord knows the way of the righteous, but the way of the ungodly *shall perish.*
—Psalm 1:5–6

During the World War of 1939–1945 I enlisted in the royal Australian Air Force. I was sent to the Air Training base at Point Cook, near Melbourne, along with all of the other new recruits. We spent our first week in what was known as the *bull ring*. A flight sergeant with a very powerful and biting voice stood in the middle of a wind swept field and drilled us from morning until night. His bawling voice could be heard well beyond the parade ground.

We were being "broken-in." We had to become obedient to any order without question or hesitation. One of the hardest things at the start was keeping in step with each other while marching. Every time a man broke step he was publicly humiliated by a lengthy berating from the sergeant. I received my fair share of his tongue-lashings.

Slowly we learned how to get back into step with a quick skip-shuffle. Much to our amazement we soon learned to keep in step with each other, and by the end of the week it seemed impossible to make a mistake.

In our walk with the Lord the *Holy Spirit* will not usually publicly expose our mistakes, which may trip us up at the beginning. He is a shepherd rather than a drill sergeant. The apostle John in his first New Testament letter shows us that our unintentional sins, committed as babes in Christ, are forgiven through Jesus Christ acting as our intercessor before our Father's throne. He writes:

> My little children [the babes] this letter I write to you so that you do not sin. But if any do sin, we have an Advocate with the Father—Jesus Christ the righteous.
>
> —1 John 2:1

My sports coach at college promised to turn me into a 200 meter champion sprinter. In my first big race I stumbled and fell, headlong, just meters from the finish.

Dear reader, you can expect that after you have been born of the Spirit and accepted the Scriptures of the Doctrine of Righteousness that you may stumble a few times as you start to run the race. However we must not get comfortable with sin and grieve the Holy Spirit. John soon puts us straight about sinning in the same letter when he warns us:

> If we say that we have fellowship with God and walk in darkness, we lie and do not live the truth.
>
> —1 John 1:6

He confirms this with:

> He who says that he knows God, and does not obey His will is a liar, and the truth is not in him.
>
> —1 John 2:4

Anyone who sins is of the devil. (See 1 John 3:8.) All unrighteousness is sin. (See 1 John 5:17.) And, whoever does not righteousness is not of God. (See 1 John 3:10.)

Sins committed in ignorance may be forgiven through the intercession of our great High Priest, Jesus Christ. However, we must be aware that unwillful sinning that we do not stop, after being pulled up by the Holy Spirit, turns easily into presumptuously mocking our Redeemer. It can become the unforgivable sin because we can thereby insult the Holy Spirit of grace. (See Hebrews 10:29.)

Paul writes:

> Be not deceived, God is not mocked; whatever a man sows that also shall he reap.
>
> —Galatians 6:7

> Without Holiness no man will see God.
> —HEBREWS 12:14

Peter and Paul do not ever say that mature Christians can have their sins forgiven. It was normal in their day to assume every Christian knew that born of the Spirit believers are fully empowered and expected by God to live righteously and be overcomers of sin. Jesus says only the overcomers can be sure that their names will not be rubbed out from the Book of Life. (See Revelation 3:5.)

Jesus told John to send a message to churches that were sinning in order to tell them to immediately repent and be overcomers or else He will come and do one of the following: remove their candlestick out of its place, hurt them by the second death, send them into great tribulation, come on them as a thief, spew them out of His mouth. (See Revelation 2:5,11, 22.) He declares to all those in the churches that He knows their works and then proceeds to warn them of His Judgments. (See Revelation 2 and 3.)

> By your righteousness that you have done you shall live.
> —EZEKIEL 18:22

All of the epistles tell us that our eternal salvation depends on living our lives righteously every day. It is not about crying *Lord, Lord*, but about doing His will. The teachings of the epistles come under what Paul calls the *word of righteousness* (the Doctrine of Righteousness). It's what this book is all about. It's about God's business. It's about doing it.

By the Spirit, we wait for the hope of righteousness by faith; nothing avails but faith working through love. (See Galatians 5:5-6.)

Peter writes:

If you have escaped the moral pollution of the world through your knowledge of the Lord and Savior Jesus Christ and again get entangled in them, and they *overcome* you, then your end is worse than before you began. In fact it would have been better not to have known *the way of righteousness* than to turn back again. Then you would fulfil the Proverb: the dog turns back to his own vomit and the washed pig to wallowing in the mud pile. (See 2 Peter 2:20–22.)

Therefore it is unscriptural and bordering on the ridiculous to teach man's theory that saints can at the same time be sinners. We either need to step in or out of step, as I quickly learned in the "*bull ring*" at Point Cook.

Paul confirms the teaching of his fellow apostle, Peter, when he writes:

> If after you have been enlightened and experienced the heavenly gift of righteousness and have been made partakers of the Holy Spirit, and if you have really tasted the good Word of God and the spiritual powers of the world to come and then fall back to sinning, then you cannot renew your repentance because your sins crucify to yourself again the Son of God and you put His name to open shame.
> —Hebrews 6:4–6

At the walled city area near the old Hong Kong airport, there is a long line of unlicensed dentist shops where everyone can see patients through the shop front windows. Toothache sufferers have to take the risk of going to these "dentists," especially the very poor.

Naturally the "dentists" must rely entirely on their reputation and not on a degree. Some shops are always full of patients while others are mostly empty. Those without a good reputation or a pleasing view through the window continue to be empty.

Many of today's churches are mostly empty. Seekers look in through the window at our works and do not like what they see. When the world sees Christians sinning or proudly confessing that they are sinners, it is no wonder they think that Christ is not a real Savior. Our sins put Him to open shame as one who cannot save.

We need to lead a righteous lifestyle in Christ where sin can be overcome.

Paul uses the following example to show that if we walk in

God's imparted righteousness we will go into Heaven; if not, our end is in Hell.

The field of earth that drinks in the recurrent rain brings forth a bumper crop and receives a blessing from God. But the field of earth that receives the same rain and yet produces a crop of thorns and briers is rejected and in the end will be burned in a fire. (See Hebrews 6:7–8.)

Finally we have the warning not to give up meeting with other Christians.

We need to continually encourage each other to love and to do *good works*, for if we sin willfully after having received the knowledge of the truth, there is no longer any forgiveness available.

The work of righteousness shall be peace, and the result of righteousness quietness and assurance forever. (See Isaiah 32:17.)

Chapter 7

Saved From What?

You love doing righteousness and you hate wickedness therefore God, thy God, has anointed thee with the oil of gladness.

—Psalms 45:7

To have gladness we need to be anointed by God with His oil of gladness. It does no good to try to produce happiness for ourselves or seek after it with drugs and the pleasures of sin.

As Christians we are God's workmanship, created in Christ Jesus to perform the *good works* God ordained for us to do. (See Ephesians 2:10.)

After World War II, there were millions of displaced and homeless people seeking a new life in a new country. Many were invited by the Australian government to come settle in my homeland. They were welcome on the condition that they would do any work they were assigned to do. Because of this, I saw qualified medical men obediently working with a pick and shovel.

Jesus Christ invited us into His kingdom of light expecting that we perform the good works that He prepared for us before the creation of the world. We were predestined to conform to the image of the Son. (See Ephesians 1:11 and Romans 8:29.)

Like the displaced people from World War II, we came in by sovereign grace, but there were conditions attached. We ignore the conditions at our own risk, even if some renowned teachers claim there are none. We must keep in mind that we are accountable for our own actions in this world and the next.

Let us have grace whereby we may serve God acceptably with reverence and godly fear. Our God is a consuming fire. (See Hebrews 12:28–29.)

God's fire both refines and punishes. It is God who made hell and also the eternal lake of fire. (See Revelation 20:14.)

The great prophet Daniel told King Nebuchadnezzar of Babylon: stop sinning, be righteous, and show mercy to the poor. (See Daniel 4:27.)

Therefore, we learn that it is God's will even for rulers to stop sinning and do good works of love. The great debate that split the church into two wings was not about the works required for salvation, but about the word *saved*.

The reformers used the word *saved* to mean that we were *reconciled to God by the blood of Christ through grace by faith*. However, the church of that time period used the word *saved* to mean *saved from God's wrath on judgment day*.

Romans 5:9–10 explains that while both views are correct, Paul prefers *saved* to mean *saved from God's final wrath*. However, he also refers to the initial experience of *being saved* by using the word *reconciliation* in the definition as understood by the church reformers of the sixteenth century.

For if, when we were enemies, we were reconciled to God by the death of His Son, much more having now been reconciled, we *shall be saved by His life*, for its no longer we who live but, Christ who lives in us. (See Romans 5:10; Galatians 2:20.)

In Ephesians 2:8–9, Paul uses the word *saved* to explain our reconciliation. Therefore, we can see that the New Testament uses the word *saved* to cover both experiences.

I believe every Christian will be pleased to know that the debate recently came to an end when the Catholic and Lutheran churches signed an official document, on behalf of their respective world-wide members, stating that the start of our salvation (reconciliation) is by grace and through faith without works.

Sitting down together in goodwill can usually resolve our misunderstandings of the other party's point of view. Whatever our point of view concerning our future salvation from God's wrath, it is clear that Jesus teaches that when He comes as Judge, he will judge on works alone. (See Romans 5:9.)

At the end of our sixth year in Japan, I received three separate prophesies over my life which directed me to go to Jerusalem.

Summer was nearly over, but it was still hot and dusty. After leaving the central post office of the modern part of Jerusalem, I had set out for home. Passing by the Damascus gate of the old walled city, I laid down two shekels for a large bunch of my favorite sun-dried *grapes*. The elderly Arab lady that manned the makeshift *fruit* stand sat on a footpath with her produce out on the pavement every day in hopes of taking home a few shekels. The sun and wind had hardened her face, but her eyes had the soft gentle glow of a grandmother. We exchanged friendly glances since I was a regular customer. I told her *todarabah—thank you* in Hebrew.

I was sweating by the time I had descended into the Kidron Valley, then climbed the steep slope to the summit of the Mount of Olives. As I paused to catch my breath, I surveyed the area for suspicious looking characters since I was well inside the P.L.O. territory known as the West Bank of Israel and inhabited mostly by Arabs.

While most were my friends, it is still a dangerous area filled with thieves. To the west I looked towards the original temple site built by King Solomon. In my mind's eye I saw Jesus sitting near me on the Mount of Olives, separated from the milling crowds, and quietly teaching His disciples. They seemed to be hanging on every word, for each word was proceeding from the mouth of God. As I drew near I heard Him saying:

"When the Son of Man shall come in His glory and all the holy angels with Him, then shall He sit on the throne of His Glory. Before Him shall be gathered people from all nationalities (down through the ages) and He shall separate them one from another as you have seen the shepherds doing. The sheep on His right hand, the goats on his left. Then to the ones on His right, the King shall say: *Come ye blessed of my Father and inherit the kingdom prepared for you from the creation of the world. Because when I was hungry you gave me food, when I was thirsty you gave me a drink. I was a stranger and you took me in, naked and you clothed me. I was in prison and you visited me.*"

He continued on, strong yet gentle: "Then shall the righteous answer Him, *but Lord, when was it that we saw you hungry and fed you? Or thirsty and gave you drink? Or when did we see you a stranger and took you in? Or naked and we gave you clothes? Or when did we see you sick and in prison and we visited you?*"

Then shall the King answer: *Truly I say to you when you did it to even one of these, the least of my brothers, you did it to me.*

Then shall He say to the ones on His left hand: (He paused for a moment and it was then that I thought I heard Him catch His breath. His voice took on a tone of sadness.) "Depart from me, you cursed ones, into everlasting fire that has been prepared for the devil and his angels. For I was hungry and you gave me no food, I was thirsting and you gave me no drink, I was a stranger but you did not open your door to me, naked and you would not clothe me, I was sick and in prison and you did not visit me."

I felt a slight shiver go down my back as He went on to say:

"Truly I say unto you that inasmuch as you did it not to one of these, the least of my brothers you did it not to me."

Those on the left will go away to everlasting punishment, but the righteous to life eternal. (See Matthew 25:31–46.)

Our King had finished speaking. I turned away as a friend called my name, and in deep thought I walked down to where I was living in the ancient town of Bethany.

Television alerts us that the starving, the sick, and the prisoners are still close to our doorsteps. If we had to come before our King today for judgment where would we stand—on His right or on His left? Or, are we presumptuously thinking that Christians do not get judged?

Perhaps we have forgotten Peter's warning to us:

If you call on the Father, who without respect of persons judges every man according to their works, then pass your short stay on this earth in fear. (See 1 Peter 1:17.)

If we compete in a sporting event and do not comply with all the rules we are not eligible to receive a gold medal. (See 2 Timothy 2:5.)

> The righteousness of the upright shall deliver them.
> —Proverbs 11:6, KJV

Let no man deceive you—only the people who *do* righteously are righteous. (See 1 John:3–7.)

You shall deliver your own soul by your righteousness. (See Ezekiel 14:20.)

As Christians, we are assured of our inheritance only if our lifestyle has been in obedience to God's will as directed by the *Holy Spirit*. (See Romans 8:1–2, 4.)

The teaching that righteousness can be lost is not new. The prophet Ezekiel warns:

When the righteous turn away from doing right and commit sin, then all of his past good deeds shall not be mentioned. In his trespasses and sins that he has committed, he shall die. (See Ezekiel 18:24.)

Chapter 8

Rio and Righteousness

I will betroth thee unto me in righteousness, in judgment, in loving kindness, and in mercies.

— Hosea 2:19

The Doctrine of Righteousness thus far has two definitions: walking free from the law of sin and sinning, and doing good works of love especially for our brothers in the body of Christ. The two go hand in hand.

Take heed unto yourself and unto the doctrine. Continue in it. By doing it you shall save yourself and those who obey it. (See 1 Timothy 4:16.)

After a redeye flight from New York, Margaret and I were only half-awake as we stood in the immigration line at the Rio de Janeiro airport. The first rays of the sun were just beginning to light up the dazzling and impressive statue of Christ that stands atop the nearby mountain. As I handed our passports to the courteous Brazilian officer, we looked forward to resting in the comfortable hotel that awaited us.

Suddenly, a frown came over the face of the once polite young officer. I became tense as I watched him flip through the pages of our well-filled passports. I thought, *surely nothing can be wrong*. But to our dismay we heard him say: "I am very sorry, but you cannot enter Brazil without a visa."

I felt sorry for my wife; I had let her down. God was again dealing with me in this area. The Holy Spirit was showing me not to trust that travel agents were always correct, especially in legal matters. I was the one ultimately responsible and accountable for my actions.

My agent told me before I left: "You do not need a visa to enter Brazil." While he was wrong, I was the party that received the unfortunate, yet righteous, judgment. Reluctantly we boarded an aircraft and endured several hours of wearisome and frustrating flight to Argentina. Our ministry invitation to Bello Horizonte would be postponed.

God will render to every man according to his deeds. He will give eternal life to those who patiently continue doing good deeds and who look forward to glory and honor. (See Romans 2:7.)

My nephew, John Higham, was selected to represent Australia in the 800 meters track and field at the Olympic games the last time they were held in Moscow. To be chosen, he had to become one of the world's top six runners and had to prove to the judges that he was legally an amateur who had never competed in any sport as a professional athlete.

Likewise, we cannot start our race as Christians until righteousness is imputed to us by God's grace. We are justified freely by His grace through the redemption that is in Christ Jesus. We are not required to prove anything to receive the King's pardon. But, once we start the race, we must obey the rules. There are no shortcuts; no runner is rewarded unless he runs lawfully. (See 2 Timothy 2:5.)

If our faith, trust, and obedience in Christ Jesus never falter then the saying *once saved always saved* holds true. If we finish the course still holding the visa of righteousness we will be welcomed into the eternal *kingdom of Jesus Christ*. (See 2 Peter 1:11.)

Peter said in 2 Peter 3:15–16 to count the long suffering of the Lord as salvation just as our beloved brother Paul also wrote. In all of his letters he spoke about it, but many misunderstood him. Unfortunately, the uneducated and unstable turn this and other Scriptures into self-destruction.

It is certain that even today many turn the meaning of the words *saved* and *grace* into self-destruction. Christ, who is long-suffering, patiently waits for the churches to get it right and to stop clinging to narrow-minded views that concern our final, eternal salvation.

Who Himself bore our sins in His own body on the tree so

that we, being dead to sins, could now live righteous lives. (See 1 Peter 2:24.)

Living righteously means to patiently continue in well doing. (See Romans 2:7.)

Chapter 9

Toronto or My Dignity?

I will take away your heart of stone, and I will give you a heart of flesh.

—Ezekiel 36:26

Think of a basket of summer fruit—delicious peaches, plums, apricots, nectarines, and avocados. But they each have a heart of unbreakable stone. If we bite too deeply into the fruit we can break a tooth.

God's prophet was moved by the Holy Spirit to tell us to be careful not to show love only on the outside, while nurturing hard hearts deep down in our souls. Paul says our hearts get hardened by unbelief and the deceitfulness of sin. (See Hebrews 3:13.)

It is the delight of the Holy Spirit to turn hard hearts into soft hearts. Imagine a peach with tender, juicy, desirable flesh throughout the fruit. This is the way He wants us to behave all of the time.

The Holy Spirit sheds God's love abroad in our hearts. (See Romans 5:5.)

It was a privilege to get caught up in a Holy Spirit revival in the Queensland town of Innisfail in the late 1970s. I saw hundreds of hearts of stone melted instantly as people opened themselves to the flow of the Holy Spirit of God. I was among the first to be wooed, and it was not long before my wife and family were also consumed with the fire of His love. Denominational lines were crossed during the revival.

We all came into the unity of the Spirit. As with all Holy Spirit revivals, there was a price that we had to pay. When the Holy Spirit falls, there is almost always a manifestation of His presence by the person speaking out and praying in what they believe is a heavenly language.

We found that heavenly languages are well documented in the New Testament book of Acts—a surprise to most of us. Praying in tongues offended many in the church, and as a result, we found ourselves cut off from most of our former friends. We were even accused of being under the devil's power.

Because the Holy Spirit continued to fill us with His love day after day, week after week, and because we all fell in love with Jesus with a consuming love previously never experienced, we all considered the defamation of men a small cost. Nothing can compete with the experience of God's glory dwelling within. American author Jack Deere later wrote a book about his own similar experience and appropriately titled it *Surprised by the Spirit*. The Spirit certainly surprised us and continues to do so.

In the mid-1990s my wife and I felt that our hearts were again growing tiny kernels of stone. In order to experience the revival in Toronto, we felt it necessary to endure the long and expensive flight. Because the revival had received a lot of criticism from *churchy* circles, I thought that we might find a genuine Holy Spirit revival of His all consuming love there.

People always react in unexpected and strange ways when the Holy Spirit pours down his refreshment. Some do not have a circuit breaker that can cope when He personally downloads His love power. When His downloads first fell on the original Christians in Jerusalem they acted like drunks, which greatly shocked the establishment. I can easily imagine the Pharisees linking the behavior of those first Christians to Satan.

Sensational happenings might have attracted some to Toronto, but for thirty days we witnessed well over ten thousand visitors swimming in the river of God's love. It was like the Innisfail Revival all over again—but at Toronto His love seemed to be more powerful and more life changing. Millions of people from nearly every denomination in the world have come away from Toronto's Airport Christian Fellowship with a refreshing of unspeakable joy and love.

I should not have been surprised when we received a less-than-warm reception at home; in every revival it has been reliably documented that the greatest critics are the ones who were in His previous revival. However, I was shocked when we experienced negativity, criticism, and lies from our own brothers and sisters in the Lord.

During our twenty-seven years of walking in the love of the Holy Spirit my wife and I have learned that He is very sensitive. He is very easily grieved and withdraws when there is a spirit of criticism. He obviously will not be placed in a box to be measured and cross-examined by mere men.

His behavior is identical to Jesus' earthly behavior. Sinning against Him is unforgivable. He will not attend a gathering that has set boundaries for Him.

The Spirit can flow in times of silence and in times of great noise. He is delighted when people's hearts are expectant and open to him in enthusiastic praise and worship.

He comes to strip us of our self-serving worldly dignity. Worldly prudence is not His way. Any friendships formed with the ways of the world make us His enemies. He shuns us when our conversations turn to worry, or coveting money and possessions. He goes out of His way to replenish generous and cheerful givers. He does not accept being mocked by repetitive sinning or deliberate *double-mindedness*. He refuses to be associated with anyone who holds on to unforgiveness.

I hope you can learn from this brief look at His character that He is not one with which to trifle. He is almighty God, the Spirit of our Father and of His Son Jesus. I serve Him daily.

Hebrews 3:13 warns us to exhort each other daily lest anyone be hardened by the deceitfulness of sin.

We are encouraged to know and believe that after we are born of the Spirit, we can have a living hope in our future inheritance because of Christ's resurrection from the dead. It is an incorruptible inheritance reserved for us in heaven. We are kept righteous and sinless for our inheritance by the power of God through *faith* until the day our salvation becomes reality. (See 1 Peter 1:4–5.)

Righteousness is walking in a relationship with the Holy

Spirit as faithfully as a loving bride walks with her husband. No longer are our desires centered on our former attractions. The things of the world fade from our sights like shadows from a midday sun. Like a young bride, our desire is to produce fruit from His love.

The Spirit and the bride continually call "come Lord Jesus," and He replies, "surely I come quickly." (See Revelation 22:17, 20.)

For I have espoused you unto one husband that I may present you a chaste virgin unto Christ. (See 2 Corinthians 11:2.)

Satan is out to besmirch marriage. We now see fornication—sex before marriage—even finding its place in the church. Jesus warned us that not long before God's patience expires, men's hearts would grow cold. I can feel the chill in the air already.

Because iniquity shall abound, the love of many shall grow cold. But he that endures until the end shall be saved. (See Matthew 24:12–13.)

Anyone who is sinning cannot claim to be born of God. *For whoever is born of God does not, and cannot, sin.* (See 1 John 3:9.)

We are *double-minded* if we claim to trust in Jesus Christ as Lord, but at the same time doubt His promise for our life: he whom the Son sets free, from committing sin, is free indeed. (See John 8:34–36.)

A *double-minded* man is unstable in all of his ways and will not receive anything that he asks from the Lord. (See James 1:7–8.)

Can we trust a bank that employs self-confessed thieves? Can we expect a person to believe and trust Christ as their Savior when Christians are self–confessed sinners, or openly living sinful lives?

God's promises may appear to be unobtainable, but Christ says we receive his promises by faith, not by sight. It is our faith in God's promises that enables us *to partake of God's nature and escape the corruption that is in the world.* (See 2 Peter 1:4.)

God's forgiveness and loving kindness flows out from everlasting to everlasting. Our sinning breaks the lifeline that connects us to His mercy and forgiveness.

Looking diligently lest there be any fornicator or sinner as Esau, who for one little morsel of pleasure sold His inheritance, and afterwards his tears of repentance were not accepted. (See Hebrews 12:16–17.)

For those who sinned were slain in the wilderness. (See Hebrews 3:17.)

Sinners condemn themselves, for they profess that they know God, but in their deeds they deny Him, being abominable and disobedient and without good *works*. (See Titus 1:16)

If we sin willfully after coming to acknowledge the truth, our lifeline cannot be reconnected. (See Hebrews 10:26–31.)

The Doctrine of Righteousness that we are learning about is very sobering. By practicing righteousness, we become the happiest people on earth. We are filled with God's love, peace, and joy in the midst of a troubled world.

However, Christ's promise to never leave us or forsake us is conditional. We must persevere in living a righteous lifestyle. He warns us that if our lifestyle is only partially righteous, He spews us out of His mouth. (See Revelation 3:16.)

When I was young, my dad had an old Ford sedan. Each morning he had to hand crank it to get it started. Recently the Holy Spirit spoke to me and said: "I have been trying to crank up the Church tirelessly over the past one hundred years. I have turned the engine over, but it will not fire up because there is water in the gasoline. It is the water of sin."

Know you not that to whom you yield yourselves slaves to obey, his slaves you are to whom you obey; whether of sin unto death, or of obedience unto righteousness. (See Romans 6:16.)

Chapter 10

Friend—Stay Healed

We being dead to sin should live unto righteousness.
—1 Peter 2:24

Imagine walking into a Christian meeting with your dear wife only to find a naked man cooking a meal over a fire of human dung at the front of the room. The Holy Spirit once commanded holy men of God to do just that. (See Isaiah 20:2–3; Ezekiel 4:12.) How would you react if you saw such a display in your church?

Without doubt most would run outside, never to return. There would be loud cries of protest that the Holy Spirit is too much of a gentleman to arrange or approve of such an occurrence. Men would use their pulpits to denounce that such actions are from Satan. Without even thinking about it, they would risk blaspheming the Holy Spirit.

God by His Spirit can do wild things to get our hardened hearts back on track. What is coming out of your mouth about what is happening at the front of the room in Toronto, Pensacola, and Smithfield?

The mouth of the righteous is a well of life. (See Proverbs 10:11.)

The Prophet Obed warned King Asa: "If you draw close to God, He will draw close to you. However, if you turn away from Him, He will turn away from you." (See 2 Chronicles 15:2.)

Paul tells us: Come, let us put on the brand new man that God created in His righteousness and true holiness. (See Ephesians 4:24.)

Who is the brand new man of God? Is he the result of the Holy Spirit working in him for endless years as he trudges along carrying his cross like a true martyr, and making sure everyone knows about it?

No, he is a scriptural, born-of-the-Spirit believer who carries in unspeakable joy his imputed righteousness from his spiritual birthday. He steps out in faith and exchanges his own life for Christ's life.

That man has nothing to brag about; his life works are gifts from *God*. In Him the man lives righteously and is not hidden from God. Before God he is open and exposed, yet he is not ashamed. He is humbled because it is Christ's life and no longer his own.

In the *Spirit*, we are no longer fallen Adam-men but Christ-men.

The Bible carries the Doctrine of Righteousness like a river flowing through thirsty ground. It is fulfilled in the life of Jesus Christ. He is righteousness personified; the author and the finisher of it. The letters of his first apostles faithfully expound it.

He was wounded for our sins, bruised for our iniquities, and by the whipping He received, we were healed. (See Isaiah 53:5.)

When Christ suffered and died as a sacrifice to His Father on our behalf, we were healed of the disease of sin. Sin was a disease, like leprosy, that was destroying us, leading to spiritual death.

We were healed by our own death with Christ's death. (See Romans 6:6.) Death not only heals us from physical diseases but also from sin. (See Romans 6:7.) A sensible person that is healed from a contagious disease takes special care not to become infected again

How can we be sure that we will never again contract the deadly disease of sin? Certainly we are continually going to be tempted to do so. As mentioned in chapter one, the Holy Spirit healed me from asthma twenty-seven years ago. I received a promise from the Lord that the disease would never return. I have walked in that promise, and it has come true.

One day, when I was still learning the Doctrine of Righteousness and living in Japan, I was sitting on the verandah of our house as the hot afternoon sun of August was giving way to the cool of the evening. Dreaming, I was startled by Ine

Kusubae, a little barefoot Japanese grandmother from next door. She had a gentle voice, but as she spoke I could detect a note of urgency bordering on panic. "Geoff *san* please help," she said. *San* is a term of respect.

Speaking to me slowly in Japanese, she explained that she and her husband were taking care of their two grandsons for the weekend. One of the boys had doubled over on their floor because he was suffering a terrible and frightening asthma attack. She explained that it was one of the rare days when even the pharmacies were closed, and the nearest doctor could not be contacted.

The village of Tachiwana had been her home all of her life. As a young girl her job had been to carry the water supply to her home in buckets from the mountain stream that flowed down the center of the valley. In the growing season she knew how to open the small sluice gates and turn the water on the rice paddies that were laid out like a patchwork quilt through the valley.

Since the war, she had been married to a local farmer and had seen the asphalt roads, reticulated water, and electricity change the lifestyle of the farmers. However, they would not relinquish their traditional religion of Buddhism. It is built into their culture. Buddhism teaches them never to let their emotions influence their life in any way. They recognize that in their flesh lives no good thing and they suppress the flesh by suppressing emotions.

Everyone who watches television will have noticed the inscrutable faces of the Orientals in the Far East. At funerals ladies are not allowed to cry, but many times one would turn into our home as the procession moved out of site. Once inside, she would bury her head into my wife's shoulder and weep freely.

It is understandable that the boxed-up emotions, held from early childhood, often cause men and women as young as forty to die suddenly in the street. To help relieve the tension, many families beat a straw stuffed dummy that they have hanging in their homes.

Now a grandmother, Ine Kusubae spends her days working in her son's computer chip factory in a nearby town. But only yesterday, from sun up to sun down, I watched her picking stones out of her beloved rice paddy that lie dormant between our houses. Like all Japanese ladies she was only slightly built, but extremely strong. She had learned patience through obedience. They wear no jewelry or ornaments but recognize the inner qualities of the quiet and gentle spirit of which Paul writes.

Kitte kudasai she whispered as she left our verandah. I assured her that I would indeed *come soon*. For several hours, my wife and I prayed that in the name of Jesus, the boy would be healed. In the room, there was the usual altar stacked with small idols and fruit, an offering for the Buddha statue. We sensed a battle was taking place in the spiritual realm.

When we left the house that evening the boy was sleeping, but the wheezing continued. As we got ready to go to sleep, I told Margaret that I felt that Jesus has let us down. I was feeling very low. In those days I had not yet come into the knowledge of what is required to walk in the Spirit. I was still learning about the Doctrine of Righteousness and so God was showing me where I was in my faith walk in Him. Like a spoiled child, I expected Him to do it in my time instead of His timing.

I was awakened early the next morning by the sounds of young boys happily throwing stones. I was acutely aware that our little patient would not be sharing in the delights of their game. I threw back the curtains to make sure that the stones were not landing on our tiny lawn and the first person I saw was our asthmatic neighbor. He was leading the attack on the make believe enemy.

Praise the Lord! *Lord I'm sorry I doubted you and your timing.* The best part is that the boy was completely healed from asthma.

The *good news* is that Jesus not only healed us spiritually and physically on His cross, but He keeps us healed in His resurrected life. (See John 8:34, 36.)

He sends into us the *Spirit of life* that gives us a lifestyle free from sin. We are freed from a punishment of death. (See Romans 8:2.)

We shall be saved by His life (at the judgment in the future). (See Romans 5:10.)

Nothing and nobody else is needed; for He who started a good work in you is well able to complete it. (See Philippians 1:6.)

We will be re-infected with sin unless we believe those promises of God and act on them in faith. We are given great and precious promises so that we can partake in the divine nature of Christ. (See 2 Peter 1:4.) Romans 8:29 is an example of one of these great and precious promises. It says that we who are called were predestined to conform to the image of God's Son, Jesus.

The righteous shall flourish like a palm tree and grow like a cedar. (See Psalm 92:12.)

Chapter 11

Professor Cho and Overcoming Sin

In every nation the one who fears Him and does righteousness is accepted with Him.
—Acts 10:35

On the way to Kagoshima, the southern volcano city on Kyushu Island in Japan, we first flew from Cairns, Queensland, into Tokyo's Narita Airport. Placing our trust in the Lord, we had not arranged a place for our overnight stay. Instead, we had agreed to allow Jesus to lead us by His Spirit.

Feeling stiff, we walked out of the plane, through the tunnel to the reception floors, and noticed that the sun was having a last glimpse of Japan as it slipped down behind the endless line of rice paddies. Finding myself beside a well-dressed Asian gentleman I managed, with some effort, to catch his eye. Taking a deep breath I said slowly in English: *Excuse me, but do you know of a cheap* ryokan (hotel) *that is close to this airport?*

His expression did not change, and I was not surprised when he turned on his heel and walked on. Another thirty paces and he stopped in our path, turned to me and said: "Why you come Japan?"

I replied: "We are here to tell the people about Jesus."

Without a reply he strolled past the line of four hundred Japanese tourists. Another fifty paces and again he stopped us in our tracks. With the faintest hint of a twinkle in his eye, I heard him say those famous words: "Follow me."

He purchased our rail tickets and took us through the maze of Tokyo's underground system that includes color-coded trains and stations at various levels. It seemed like hours before we emerged again at street level. Faithfully following him we squeezed into a small taxi with our backpacks on our laps and drove through endless dark and narrow roadways. It was after midnight when we gathered our packs and climbed, in inky darkness, a vertical steel ladder attached to a building of some sort.

When we reached the small landing, our guide tapped on the door and it swung open. In a blaze of warm light we were welcomed with outstretched arms by a pleasant, middle aged, round-faced woman. It turned out that our dear guide was Professor Cho, a Korean who had accepted an appointment at the prestigious University of Tokyo. Our host family, also Koreans, were his lifelong friends. They had a lucrative car repair business downstairs.

We were immediately treated like royalty and invited persistently to stay with them, free of charge, for the next twelve months. I tried to communicate that we were on our way to do the Lord's business in Kagoshima. After a few days I was able to lead Professor Cho to Jesus. We stayed with them as royal guests for a week.

It snowed heavily the afternoon before we left. Early the next morning our hostess went to the shops and bought us warm scarves, jackets, and snowsuits.

As we said farewell at the station my wife turned to me with tears in her eyes and said: "The Lord surely leads us to lie down in green pastures when we really trust in Him."

> For our heart shall rejoice in him, because we have trusted in his holy name.
> —Psalm 33:21, KJV

Yes, when we get out of the way, the Holy Spirit will do His work.

Our God truly loves us and wants us to recognize His love gifts which He gives to us. We must be careful to not reject Him by not accepting that in Him it is impossible for sin to get back into our house. In Him we are an impregnable fortress. That is GRACE!

There is no way we can get around the many New Testament

Scriptures that promise us we are set free from sinning in Him. Are we going to wait another two thousand years before we will place our trust in Him and fill our mouths with His promises? The purpose of this book is to stir up and challenge Christians to walk in the promises of Christ our Lord. Yes, persecution will follow. Look at history.

The Jews killed the Lord Jesus and their own prophets, and persecuted the first Christians. (See 1 Thessalonians 2:15.)

Persecution often comes from within the fold. I am not too upset about persecution for my joy and crown of rejoicing will be to see all of us in the presence of our Lord Jesus Christ at His coming. (See 1 Thessalonians 2:19–20.) As soon as we respond to His call, we are charged to lead a lifestyle worthy of God, one that He requires if we are to see His kingdom and glory. (See 1 Thessalonians 2:11–12; 1 Peter 1:17.)

For God has not called us to sinful behavior, but to holiness. If we disregard God's will, we insult not man, but God who gave us His Holy Spirit. (See 1 Thessalonians 4:7–8.)

Chapter 12

Atom Bomb and Cannot Sin

On a hill close to the city center of Nagasaki stands a memorial to twenty-one Japanese Christian men who were crucified by the authorities in the seventeenth century. Interestingly, it is almost directly over this hill that the second atomic bomb exploded in 1945.

> Be not deceived; God is not mocked: for whatsoever a man soweth, that shall he also reap.
> —Galatians 6:7, KJV

Jesus taught:

> If any man will come after me, let him deny himself, and take up his cross…whosoever will save his life shall lose it.
> —Matthew 16:24–25, KJV

He was warning the disciples that self must vacate the throne. Paul takes us a step further by reminding Christians that our cross is a memorial of the crucifixion and death of our old carnal man who died with Christ in the crucifixion. But if we do not accept by faith that the carnal (flesh) man has died, we will find our (self) carnal man wants to keep carrying the cross as a sort of penance or as a "dying to self daily" attitude. No! The cross has become a memorial of our forgiveness and our *death*. Paul says, "ask yourself the question, how can we who have died to sin live any longer therein?" (Rom. 6:2, author's paraphrase). The answer, of course, is we cannot! When you can say "I cannot sin," you will have accepted chapter six to the Roman church, *otherwise you have rejected it.*

Both of these desires (penance and dying daily) belong to the old carnal man and are unscriptural. When Paul used the expression "I die daily," he was referring to himself as willingly accepting being a target of persecution for his faith. (See 1 Corinthians 15:30–32.)

It has nothing to do with dying to self for Paul knew, as we should, that dead men cannot die again. Most of the world's religions teach that if man is to be good enough to get into a heaven he needs to die to self. Christianity on the other hand teaches rightly that man can achieve nothing—otherwise Christ died in vain.

In Christ we died to self, and for all time. But the just are just because of their *faith*. (See Romans 1:17.) In Christ we live in complete victory if we persevere in faith. Christianity is not about *trying* to do it. It is about *faith* in Christ's ongoing victory over sin. It is no longer I that lives, but Christ who lives in me. (See Galatians 2:20.)

We are dead and our life is hid with Christ in God. (See Colossians 3:3.)

If each Christian were confessing this truth in faith, then the church would soon reflect the true *glory of God in the face of Jesus Christ*. (See 2 Corinthians 4:6.) I believe that the greatest hindrance to accepting our past death is that until we do so, our old man flesh is still on the throne. Show me a man who will not accept or does not know the Scripture that He has died, and I will show you a self-confessing sinner. (See Romans 6:2; 6:11–13.)

I believe that we are commanded to carry the cross in our minds as an ever-present reminder that we have died. Paul teaches us to offer our bodies as living sacrifices and that we shouldn't be conformed to this world. In this way our minds are renewed. (See Romans 12:1–2.)

It takes courageous faith to offer our own dear physical body as a living sacrifice. Jesus and His mother are two good examples of people that offered their own bodies as living sacrifices and then discovered the perfect will of God in their lives. Mary knew that she would at the very least be a social outcast if she became pregnant before her marriage, but she replied to God's angel "be it done unto me according to thy word"!

It is helpful to recall that to be absent from the body means to be present with the Lord. When we offer our body we must offer it even to the point that the Lord may take us through death, even as He took Peter and Paul. We must be willing to remain in His will.

Knowing that while we are at home in the body we are absent from the Lord—but we are confident and willing to be absent from our body and to be present with the Lord. (See 2 Corinthians 5:6–8.)

While in the physical realm, I am manifested through my body of flesh and blood. When my body ceases to breathe, it dies. Then I live on in the spiritual realm outside my corpse. If I die in righteousness I will then be present with the Lord.

On resurrection day when Christ returns, I will receive a new body that is incorruptible and immortal. (See 1 Corinthians 15:53.) On that day, my body is redeemed in the salvation that is my current hope. It is the day when God adopts me into the glorious liberty of the children of God. (See Romans 8:21–24.) My new body will enable me to live in the new heavens and the new earth.

My body is buried a natural body; it is raised a spiritual body. There is a natural body and there is a spiritual body. (See 1 Corinthians 15:44.)

Paul describes our resurrection when Christ returns:

For the Lord shall descend from heaven with a shout, with the voice of the archangel, with the trumpet of God. The Christians who persevered unto death shall rise first, closely followed by the Christians who are still alive. These will be changed in the twinkling of an eye from flesh bodied men into spiritual bodied men. They shall all be caught up together in the clouds to meet the Lord in the air, and they will be with the Lord forever. (See 1 Thessalonians 4:16–17; 1 Corinthians 15:52.) God shall wipe away all tears from our eyes, and there shall be no more death, neither sorrow, nor crying, nor pain. (See Revelation 21:4.)

Christ took our physical *body* to death through His death on the cross. Through His death, we can continue to live by faith without sin in order to obtain our inheritance as children of

God. (See Romans 6:6; 1 Peter 1:4–5; Colossians 3:3–4; Romans 8:4.)

Not far from the center of Rome you can go on a daily guided tour of the Catacombs, a series of tunnels where Christians who suffered persecution lived and were buried. It was a remarkable experience for my wife and I as we were led for more than an hour through a maze of dimly lit passages with niches in the walls where they had placed the dead bodies of the saints.

The remains of some bodies have not been removed and can be seen through an enclosed glass case. One was that of a child. All that remained were the bones and hair.

Our group was brought into a small room. Before our guide took us back up to the surface, he gave us a gentle and simple homily on the future resurrection of the saints and the second resurrection. His New Testament Scripture certainly cheered us.

But while our small in stature, but bold in God, priest and guide told us that we would all have to face death one day, I noticed a lady becoming agitated. She finally blurted out: "When do we take around the collection box?" She was insinuating that she did not want to hear what she considered to be a church sermon.

In the dimly lit passage, I replied: "Maybe you don't like hearing the truth." This statement broke the dam of emotions inside of her. She started crying and could not stop. Climbing the steps back into warm sunlight, she drew close to us. Between sobs, she apologized for what she called "nasty comments." I sensed that there was joy in heaven that day as another stray sheep came back to the Shepherd.

> And as he reasoned of righteousness, temperance, and judgment to come, Felix trembled.
> —Acts 24:25, KJV

Chapter 13

Beat Every Temptation

Forasmuch then as Christ hath suffered (died) for us in the flesh, arm yourselves likewise with the same mind: for he that hath suffered (died) in the flesh hath ceased from sin.

—1 Peter 4:1, kjv

Peter's teaching on freedom from sin by our death in Christ is often misunderstood because he uses the word *suffering* to stand for *death*. The key to the passage is to read five verses earlier in his letter:

Christ also hath once suffered for sins … being put to death in the flesh…

—1 Peter 3:18, kjv

I suffered in the flesh with the disease of asthma for forty-six years, but it did not stop me from sinning. I have never met anyone who claims that any form of suffering has set them free from sin. It is unscriptural to say that any suffering, apart from death, sets us free from sin.

In the above Scripture, Peter is simply confirming Paul's word to us: he who is dead is freed from sin. He says to reckon yourself dead to sin and alive to God in Christ Jesus. (See Romans 6:7, 11.)

Thank God I stopped sinning for a short while after the Holy Spirit filled me, and I began to walk in the Spirit. After twenty-seven years of learning from the Holy Spirit, I now know that I am truly dead to sin and alive to God in Christ Jesus. I have been brought out from slavery to sin and into slavery to righteousness. (See Romans 6:17–18.)

In church we may enjoy singing, "It's no longer I that lives but Christ who lives in me." But, if we continue committing sins it shows that we do not really believe it.

I suppose that at times we are all guilty of only parroting Scripture. We instead are challenged to *confess* them. Several elderly Jewish Rabbis in Jerusalem explained to me that in Hebrew, the scriptural term *confess* means to declare with our mouth a belief that is already deeply rooted and settled in our innermost being. It is an audible expression of our deepest convictions.

Speaking aloud our belief brings life to our faith.

Every day I carry my cross by confessing: "I am crucified with Jesus." (See Romans 6:6.)

Every temptation to sin is quickly overcome when I confess: "I am dead to sin and alive to God in Christ Jesus." (See Romans 6:11.) I am confessing a truth that has finally taken root in my inner being. At that confession, temptation has to flee. I can assure you that it works. It must for it is in the *Bible*. I do not have to be fearful of finding myself in places of temptation for I am an overcomer. I can do all things and go anywhere in Christ Jesus the great overcomer. Let me assure you there is no other action that will overcome temptation, although volumes have been vainly written on the steps we need to take to resist and avoid temptations. I can assure you that temptations will never cease in this life. The thief who was once a guest in our house will never stop knocking on the door and windows seeking reentry. Even when I preach the message of this book, I am many times challenged by rapping on the material windows and doors of the buildings we are in. It is one of the ways that the demons try to distract both the audience and me.

Those Scriptures written by the apostles contained the powerful promises that only became available after Golgotha and the Pentecost. Try using them to overcome temptations that come your way. I do—and it works.

Salvation is from faith to faith. This means I need to have a persevering, ongoing lifestyle that finds me *confessing* my belief in Christ and His promises.

For the righteousness of God is revealed from faith to faith.

(See Romans 1:17.)

My life in Christ is victorious when I believe and *confess* Christ's promise that the law of the *Spirit* of life in Christ Jesus has set me free from the law of sin. (See Romans 8:2.)

He can do more than we can imagine for we are complete in Him. (See Colossians 2:10.)

Can you imagine God sending His angels to help you in everyday situations?

Standing on a platform at the bottom level of the underground rail system in London, Margaret and I were in a state of exhaustion on that day in June. Constant travel and jet lag eventually takes its toll on the human body.

We were to be in Blackpool that afternoon for the National Convention of the Full Gospel Businessmen. To catch the Blackpool train we had to climb three steep and long flights of stairs. At our feet stood a pile of luggage. I looked up and down the platform, hoping for a porter. There was not a soul in sight. While I am not one to concede easily, I turned to my wife and said: "I give up, I cannot carry those bags another step."

When I said the words "I give up," the Holy Spirit was free, at last, to take over.

Suddenly, seemingly out of nowhere, two strong young men in smart gray business suits appeared and, without speaking, picked up our heavy bags and began to briskly climb the stairs. As we struggled to keep up with them I called out: "We are going to platform eleven."

Over their broad shoulders they called back: "Yes, we know." As they climbed, they chatted with each other, though I could not understand them. They were handsome and had the pink cheeks of young Englishmen.

After arriving at platform eleven they put down our luggage. We turned to thank them, but they were gone. They simply disappeared.

My wife and I believe they were angels from God. It was affirmation that He takes an interest in the small trials of our everyday lives. When we have done all we can, stand and see that the Lord is good. (See Ephesians 6:13; Exodus 14:13.)

The victorious Christian life flows from a day-by-day walk of faith in the law of the *Spirit of life in Christ Jesus*. I do everything without having to run a check on my next word or action because in trusting faith I know that the *Spirit of Jesus Christ* is living His life through mine. I freely confess my inner conviction of the biblical truth that: the law of the spirit of life in Christ Jesus has—from the day I received the *Spirit*—set me free from the law of sin.

He can do more than I can ever imagine for I am complete in Him. (See Colossians 2:10.)

God has promised eternal life only to the person who perseveres in doing righteousness. (See Romans 2:7.)

The wrath of God will be revealed against all that hold the truth in unrighteousness. (See Romans 1:18.)

God's wrath is a consuming fire. (See Numbers 16:35.)

We who were once God's enemies, because of wicked sinful works, He has now reconciled in the body of His flesh through death, to present us holy and blameless in His sight if we persevere in faith working through love. (See Colossians 1:22–23; Galatians 5:5–6.)

John is known as the apostle of love. But he does not pull any punches when He teaches us that "all unrighteousness is sin." (See 1 John 5:17.)

This confirms the teachings of the prophet Ezekiel that God sees His people as either righteous or sinners according to their ways (works). (See Ezekiel 18:25–30.) It is not about how we see ourselves. Perhaps you still see yourself as a saint and a sinner! Verse 30 sums it up where the prophet speaking on behalf of God states: "Therefore will I judge you, O house of Israel, everyone according to his ways, saith the Lord God. Repent and turn from all your transgressions; so iniquity shall not be your ruin." John writes to Christians: "In this the children of God are manifest, and the children of the devil. Whoever does not righteousness is not of God…" (See 1 John 3:10.) We are required to know that righteousness and sin are as opposite as God and the devil. Jesus says be either a saint or a sinner for a mixture of the two He will spew out of His mouth. He uses the words hot or cold to represent a saint's walk and a sinner's walk. (See Revelation 3:15–16.)

The Doctrine of Righteousness that I write about defines the way of the righteous lifestyle—its start, its course, and its finish.

It may be considered rude and offensive if we tell Christians that continue to sin that they are of the devil, but it is scriptural. (See 1 John 3:8.)

Paul writes to those of us who desire to obey God and to walk in the way of righteousness that we must live the "exchanged life" of walking in the Holy Spirit. (See Romans 8:4.) This walk in the Spirit is the opposite of walking according to the lusts of the flesh.

We find an example of the lusts of the flesh in Paul's letter to the believers in the church at Colossae. He lists them as sex outside of lawful marriage, excessive passions, love of money and possessions, wrath, malice, blasphemy, dirty talk, lies, wives who do not submit to their husbands, husbands who do not love their wives, and employees that do not obey their bosses. (See Colossians 3:5–22.)

These examples of the lusts of the flesh are not listed for us as a set of laws to be learned so as to be righteous. No—it is the Holy Spirit who gives us our righteous way of life. It is a life that is opposed to all lusts of the flesh.

I find the lusts of the flesh to be infinitely variable and so subtle that they cannot be contained in human memory. Even if we could memorize them, they would only serve to condemn us. They cannot set us free.

Anyone who is under moral law is also under the "law of sin," which makes them sin against their own will. (See Romans 7:14–23.) Anything we do that does not come under the umbrella of loving God and loving our neighbor is a lust of the flesh.

Thanks belong to the Lord Jesus as our flesh went to death with Him on the cross. (See Romans 6:6–11.) It should be noted that sin was not taken to death on the cross. Sin was forgiven on the cross. On the cross, atonement was made for our past sins and we became reconciled to God. But that is only a part of the victory. We were also freed from the power of sin. But how? Paul and Peter go to great lengths to teach us in their letters that a human being is set free from being a slave of sin by physical death, *not by the death of sin*. Paul wrote: "He that is dead is freed from sin" (Rom. 6:7, KJV). Can the verse, if you imagine yourself dead to sin, mean that sin is dead? And notice he did not say as good as dead. No! He says *dead*. (See Romans 6:11.) Can the verse, "we that are dead to sin", mean that sin is dead? (See Romans 6:2.) Can the verse, he who has died to sin, mean that sin is dead? (See Romans 6:7.) Can the verse, "you are dead", mean that sin is dead? (See Colossians 3:3.) Where did the teaching come from that mistakenly declares that sin is dead or that sin died where the blood fell? It must have originated in the mind of man for it is not in the Bible. It was sin that put our Jesus on the cross. Jesus did not put sin to death on the cross. No! It was us He took to death, for we were crucified with Jesus. (See Galatians 2:20.) There is only one mention of sin being dead in the entire Bible (see Romans 7:8), but it is talking about sin being *as good as dead* for Paul is telling us before God had given any law to mankind. But in Romans 5:13, Paul taught that up until the law sin *was in the world*. Dear reader, I will not have achieved the purpose of this book, which is to restore righteous living to the church, if I have not made it clear that sin is *not dead*. On the contrary, the Bible teaches that sin is a slave master, and the only way that we can be freed from that master is by death. Jesus therefore took our physical body to death with His death. (See Romans 6:17–18, 6.) Sin cannot be killed—*that's biblical*. Sins can be forgiven—*that's Bible*. You may be feeling that it is not all that important to know that sin is not dead and that my old carnal man is dead. But the truth is that if sin is dead, you can leave the door of your house open for the thief is no longer a threat to your eternal life. I believe with all my heart that sin is a horrible living monster who destroys us if we let him in. And I believe that the church is in a shockingly immoral and sinful condition today because we have sown for five hundred years that we can be a saint and a sinner. We reap what we sow. The great teacher John Bevere has written finish to the deception in the church that *grace* gives us a carte blanche permission to sin and not be punished with death eternal. Any Christian who returns to the way of the flesh will not inherit the kingdom of God. (See Galatians 5:21.) The judgment of God is according to truth and against those who do such things. (See Romans 1:29–32; Romans 2:2.)

My dear mother often had occasion to tell me that the road to hell is paved with good intentions. Many Christians are taught and believe that their life is going to be a series of defeats. They have the "good intention" of repenting every night and starting fresh the next morning. But unintentionally they deny themselves Jesus' promise that said: the one whom the Son sets free from sinning is free indeed. (See John 8:34–36.)

We, God's people, throughout history seem to have a weakness for preferring the traditions of men over the promises of God. God's Word says that anyone who abides in Jesus Christ does not sin, for whoever sins has not seen Him or known Him. (See 1 John 3:6.)

In my own life I can bear witness that until *I thirsted with all my heart for the Holy Spirit to fall on me in a spiritual baptism*, even though I believed I was Christian, I had not really seen Him or known Him. I was like those Samaritans who were converted by the ministry of Philip but did not receive the Holy Spirit until some time later. From experience I know that a large proportion of Christians, although converted believers and water-baptized, have not yet had the Holy Spirit come upon them. It is a real experience. Jesus does it when He sees we are so thirsty that we will ask it from Him without any of our own conditions attached. Once again, try it—you'll like it.

It is a spiritual seeing, a spiritual knowing, which wells up from within. It takes place after Jesus baptizes a person with the Holy Spirit.

I had believed in Jesus Christ as my Lord and Savior for forty-two years before the great day when He gave me the gift of the Holy Spirit. Finally I saw Him and knew Him. Now I understand the New Testament Scripture:

"But ye are not in the flesh, but in the Spirit, if so be that the Spirit of God dwell in you. Now if any man have not the Spirit of Christ, he is none of his" (Rom. 8:9).

For forty-two long years I thought I was walking in the light, but I was actually walking in darkness. I was under the misconception that I could be a saint and a sinner at the same time.

As the Scripture says:

> If we say that we have fellowship with him, and walk in darkness, we lie, and do not the truth.
> —1 JOHN 1:6, KJV

The New Testament writers do not teach that we are to repent daily. What they do teach is to awaken to righteousness and sin not, for to sin is shameful and displays that we do not have the knowledge of God's truth. (See 1 Corinthians 15:34.)

Genuine repentance is this: If your eye causes you to sin, pluck it out.

John baptized with the baptism of repentance, but you are baptized in the name of the Lord Jesus. (See Acts 19:3–4.)

John the Baptist told the Sadducees and the Pharisees that they were like snakes that needed to flee from the wrath to come—their deeds did not match their words of repentance. (See Matthew 3:7–8.)

Jesus says that just persons need no repentance. (See Luke 15:7.)

Our God-given faith has justified us as Christians, and we walk justly by the power of the Spirit of life in Christ Jesus. (See Romans 3:24; 8:2.) He is more than able to keep us from falling. (See Jude 24.)

> Fear not, little flock; for it is your Father's good pleasure to give you the kingdom.
> —LUKE 12:32, KJV

Paul reminded the Jewish converts to be careful when they became Christians not to reach the place where sinning had no place of repentance—even if like Esau, it is sought with tears. (See Hebrews 12:16–17.)

> And now, little children, abide in him; that, when he shall appear, we may have confidence, and not be ashamed before him at his coming.
> —1 John 2:28, kjv

Chapter 14

A Big Toe and Balance

Preach the word—reprove, rebuke, and warn with all long-suffering and doctrine. For the time will come when they will not listen to sound doctrine. But, after their own desires they shall gather together those teachers who tickle the ears that itch; and they shall turn away their ears from the truth. (See 2 Timothy 4:2–4.)

We can rest assure that this Doctrine of Righteousness that we are studying will not tickle our flesh.

It was a dark night. The streetlights were dim and there was a chill in the air. I snuggled under the blankets in my son's guest room in Sydney. There was no need to lower the blinds for this was a quiet and respectable suburb.

Drifting off to sleep I was thinking about two nights before when the elders of a church in the state of Victoria had stopped me from preaching the word of righteousness and ordered me to leave. In the darkness I was asking, *Lord I wonder why they invited me in the first place?*

I slept soundly, but was suddenly awakened. It was still dark, but outside my window I could see the silhouette of a man. He was obviously possessed, for he was screaming at the top of his voice, "Why don't you leave me alone?" He kept saying the phrase over and over.

My faith failed me, and instead of rebuking him in the name of Jesus, I hid my head under the blankets and broke out in a cold sweat due to fear and embarrassment. After what felt like hours, but was actually minutes, he walked off. I gathered up enough courage to look out my window and noticed that there were lights on in neighboring houses. He had certainly caused a stir. God was testing my faith in those days and it obviously was still weak.

It was a new and horrifying experience for me to see a

demon-possessed man. Today I have come to expect these reprisals of Satan. They are always horrible, but I can now, confidently in faith, stand against them in the name of Jesus.

Following any public teaching about our freedom from sinning granted to us by Jesus, I always come under attack from Satan.

I remember vividly one night on the island of Espiritu Santo in the Republic of Vanuatu in the Southwest Pacific. I had been invited as the main speaker at the annual crusade by the president of the Christian Mission Centre which is the indigenous church in that nation of islands which were once the headquarters of General MacArthur. While it is a nation that acknowledges Jesus Christ in its constitution, black magic and witchcraft are still present and with power.

Having finished a series of meetings attended by hundreds, my brother in Christ and I retired to our beds. Within minutes a pack of large dogs assembled outside our window and howled like wolves. It was a blood-curdling sound.

I saw my friend disappear under his bedclothes. Without a sound, I followed suit and hid in my bed. While we both prayed for safety, the dogs continued to howl for several hours. Sometimes we could hear them pawing at the window—the only thing separating us from the demon–possessed pack. By God's mercy and through our prayers, they finally left us alone. Once again my faith at that time was still low.

I have found that Satan tolerates most of my preaching. However, he adamantly attacks me when I teach about how to be set free in Christ from sinning.

In Jerusalem, the Jews threatened to stone me unless my street preaching stopped. However, by this time my faith had grown stronger and I continued preaching there. I avoided possible death by moving from place to place. The word of righteousness is a slap in the face to Satan. It defeats all his attempts to overcome us.

In his letters to us, the apostle John always teaches that whoever is born of God does not sin—and the wicked one touches him not. (See 1 John 5:18.)

In Toronto, I had a vision of a foot in a wool sock. It was neat and tidy, except that the big toe was sticking out through a hole in the sock. A few days later, I learned that the big toe's main function is balance.

The Lord impressed on me that in the body of Christ, I am just like a big toe. My function is to help keep the body balanced. As I write this, it is the third year of the twenty-first century, and in general, the church is leaning heavily on God's goodness and putting little weight on *His severity*.

However, there are seventy-four chapters in the New Testament epistles that warn us of His severity. They also serve to remind us that God treats disobedience as unbelief. (See 1 Peter 2:7–8.)

> For if God spared not the natural branches, take heed lest he also spare not thee. Behold therefore the goodness and severity of God: on them which fell, severity; but toward thee, goodness, if thou continue in his goodness: otherwise thou also shalt be cut off.
> —ROMANS 11:21–22, KJV

Paul knew that he could lose his inheritance by returning to the way of the flesh when he wrote:

> But I keep under my body, and bring it into subjection: lest that by any means, when I have preached to others, I myself should be a *castaway*.
> —1 CORINTHIANS 9:27, KJV, EMPHASIS ADDED

My athletic coach always insisted that the only way I could win sprinting races would be to improve my balance. It's good spiritual advice too: unbalanced Christians will easily trip and fall, and sinners cannot be winners.

The usual reason used to discredit the biblical teaching of the word of righteousness is found in 1 John 1: 8–10.

> If we say that we have no sin we deceive ourselves and the truth is not in us. If we confess our sins, He is

faithful and just to forgive us our sins and to cleanse us from all unrighteousness. If we say that we have not sinned we make Him a liar, and His word is not in us.

—1 John 1:8–10, kjv

At first glance, these verses may appear to contradict the remainder of his letter. But, when we examine the Scripture in the light of the whole New Testament teachings, including the other 102 verses of John's first epistle, we find that these three verses are obviously referring to a person's sinful condition before having been born of God by His *Spirit*. He is simply referring to what Christians often call "the sinners' prayer."

John clarifies the true meaning of these verses when he continues on in the same letter.

Anyone who sins is of the devil. (See 1 John 3:8.)

This letter is written so that you will not sin. (See 1 John 2:1.)

Anyone born of God cannot sin. (See 1 John 3:9.)

Those teachers who claim that the correct translation of the Greek should read "not go on sinning" only reinforce that once we are born of God, sinning stops. However, they misuse their enlightened translation to bolster up their sinning habits by trying to persuade us that it means that every time we start sinning we will soon stop until we start sinning again and so on *ad infinitum*.

He that says "I know Him," and does not do His will, is a liar. (See 1 John 2:4.)

> If we say that we have fellowship with Him, and walk in darkness, we lie, and do not the truth.
> —1 John 1:6, kjv

> If ye know that He is righteous, ye know that everyone who doeth righteousness is born of Him.
> —1 John 2:29

Whoever abides in Christ does not sin. Whoever sins has not seen Him or known Him. (See 1 John 3:6.)

In this the children of God are manifest and the children of the devil—whoever is not righteous—is not of God. (See 1 John 3:10.)

> We know that whoever is born of God sinneth not.
> —1 John 5:18

Nowhere in the New Testament does God's Word teach us that born-again believers walking in the Spirit and abiding in Him are still sinners. At first sight, 1 John 1:8–10 could be misconstrued. But, in light of the remainder of his letter, we can see clearly that he is writing about our condition *before* we were born of God.

Frequently I come across believers who do not realize that they were truly sinners before their conversion. These Christians need to come to understand 1 John 1: 8-10 .

Coming to Christ without also believing and confessing 1 John 1:9 will not produce a righteous Christian—Christ came to save sinners. (See Matthew 9:13.) And if they do not walk in the Spirit they will not continue to be righteous. (See Romans 8:2, 4.) You were the slaves of sin, but being made free from sin you became the slaves of righteousness. How few believers go on to believe those two truths. (See Romans 6:17–18.) Therefore, is it any wonder that Jesus said, "wide is the road that leads to destruction and many are rushing down it, but narrow is the road that leads to eternal life and *few* there are who find it." (author's paraphrase; see Matthew 7:13–14.)

Only after our past sins have been forgiven can we go on to lead the overcomer's righteous life in Christ. *God has set forth Christ to be the propitiation through faith in His blood, to declare His righteousness for the remission of* past *sins*. (See Romans 3:25.)

We need a good start to run the salvation race successfully. We must know that we were sinners and that in Jesus Christ we have had them forgiven and pardoned for all time. I think it was John Landy who, after breaking the four-minute mile, said: "I don't look back, I keep my eyes on the finish."

Apostle Paul writes to us that the unwritten law of the Spirit of life in Christ Jesus has already set us free from sin and sinning. (See Romans 8:2.)

It seems that it is generally accepted that we are born of the

Spirit. However, Christians need to believe and walk in that beautiful promise, and indeed all of God's promises, that we have in Jesus Christ.

Confessing my belief in Christ's promises keeps my faith lively. Try it—you'll like it.

The tests, trials, and sufferings that come our way can never be directly used to set us free from sinning. It is only by faith in Christ and His promises; *in Him we cannot sin.*

The trials, tests, and sufferings we are going through are a means of strengthening our faith in Christ and eliminating doubts. In the end it was doubt that kept the Israelites out of the Promised Land. Their doubts led them to disobey God's promises. Satan specializes in sowing seeds of doubt in our mind. His encounter with Eve is the prime example.

> How shall we, that are dead to sin, live any longer therein?
>
> —Romans 6:2, kjv

Our answer to that question will determine our eternal future. If we believe that it is true that we have died, we will no longer be under the power of sin. If we do not believe it, we will go on sinning and God will destroy us.

Bold words, you may accuse—but Paul wrote the rest of Romans 6. It asserts that what I have just explained is scriptural and, therefore, the truth. The wages of sin is death, but our old (carnal) man was crucified with Him, and our body of sin destroyed that henceforth, we should not serve sin. (See Romans 6:6, 23.)

Paul is talking to us about our body of flesh and blood which was controlled by sin until it was crucified. This is new wine teaching and it needs a new wine skin to hold it. Are you prepared to change?

I have found, and am convinced, that Satan is determined to persuade Christians that they are still going to sin. Well meaning Christians may reply that Paul also taught in Romans 3:23: "For all have sinned, and come short of the glory of God." But Paul is here describing the condition of all of mankind *before* their spiritual birth through God.

If it were true that Paul and John were saying in one breath that, born of God, believers were set free from sinning and in the next breath that they are all still sinners, then both of those apostles would have been discarded as fools that contradict themselves. These men are not fools, but penned chapters of the Bible that are accepted as the Holy foundation of the living temple of God by all of the Christian church.

What Paul teaches is that all people are sinners under what he calls "the law of sin," *until* they become righteous by confessing their belief in Jesus and walking in the Spirit of God.

Those whom He calls He also justifies and those He justifies He also glorifies. (See Romans 8:30.)

When we were once slaves to sin we were free from righteousness. But now that we have been made free from sin and become a slave of God, we have our fruit in holiness and our end is everlasting life. (See Romans 6:20–22.)

Only those of us who do God's good works are allowed to enter the gates of the city the Bible calls the *New Jerusalem* and so receive our eternal inheritance and eat of the Tree of Life. (See Revelation 22:14.)

That we may be called trees of righteousness, the planting of the Lord that He may be glorified. (See Isaiah 61:3.)

CHAPTER 15

REFORMATION NOW

In righteousness shall you be established; no weapon formed against you shall prosper. This is the heritage of the servants of the Lord and their righteousness is in me. (See Isaiah 54:14, 17.)

Jesus fulfilled Isaiah's prophecy two thousand years ago, but today we will need a *reformation* before most of the church will accept it.

In the Old Testament the Scriptures confirm there was no one righteous, no not one. (See Romans 3:9–10.) In most churches today we hear the same story—"that none should dare lay claim to being freed from sin." If you doubt me then you can quickly find out for yourself by confessing in "church" that you believe you have been set free from sinning.

If we are not freed from sinning, then Christ died in vain. He should have just remained in heaven.

Personally I cannot see the point of being a Christian if it only means forgiveness without immediate and sustained freedom from the power of my old master, sin.

A short time after receiving the Holy Spirit and experiencing His healing power in both the physical and spiritual realm, I went with my wife to be baptized in water. The baptism took place in a crystal clear pool of the swiftly flowing Tully River in Queensland.

It was an overcast day as my brothers and sisters in Christ gathered together on the bank. As the guitar strummed the tune "This is the day," I noticed an eagle soaring overhead.

Coming up out of the waist deep water, the sun broke through the clouds to match our joy and anointing. A kingfisher even dipped his azure wings in a salute.

From that day on I experienced separation in a more powerful way. I knew for sure that I was dead to sin. Nobody told me, but later I discovered that my death is scriptural. (See Romans 6:1–11.)

I had been born of water and of the Spirit. But like the Roman Cornelius and his household, it took place in reverse order. (See Acts 10:44–48.)

First Jesus baptized me in the Holy Spirit, (see chapter one) and later one of his servants, Brian Henaway, baptized me in water.

Luke's account says that while Peter was continuing to bear witness to Jesus, the Holy Spirit fell from above upon all those listening. Peter and his Jewish friends were astonished that God had poured out the gift of the Holy Spirit on Gentiles, for they heard them all speaking in tongues and magnifying God. Then Peter declared: "Can anyone forbid that these now become baptized (in water) who also have, like us, received the Holy Spirit?" Then, he commanded them to be baptized in the name of the Lord Jesus. (See Acts 10:44–48.)

Anyone born of the Spirit of Jesus Christ is a child of God. But the Bible reminds us that to keep our position as adopted sons and daughters we have to obey the Spirit's lead. (See Romans 8: 14.)

We are God's children living in a hope that looks forward to the great day of our inheritance when Christ returns and our bodies are redeemed from the grave. Peter calls it the time when we will enter the everlasting kingdom of our Lord and Savior Jesus Christ. (See 2 Peter 1:11.) Paul refers to this time as the day of our redemption, our adoption (See Romans 8:23–24.) After that day none of us who have been reconciled can ever lose our salvation. It is then no longer a hoped-for promise, it is the irrevocable prize—the winner's crown.

Peter lists the works we need to do to make our election and calling permanent. He says to pay attention to them so we will not fall and lose our inheritance. (See 2 Peter 1:1–10.)

Add to your faith virtue; and to virtue add knowledge. To knowledge add temperance; and to temperance patience; and to patience godliness. To godliness add brotherly kindness and to brotherly kindness add love. Now if these works be in you and abound, you shall neither be unfruitful nor barren. If we lack these works we are blind and cannot see ahead and we have forgotten that our past sins have been wiped out (2 Pet. 1:5–9, author's paraphrase).

The works Peter is writing about are the works that Paul spoke of in his letter to the Ephesian church. He writes:

> For we are his workmanship, created in Christ Jesus unto good works, which God hath before ordained that we should walk in them.
> —Ephesians 2:10, kjv

It is very important that we do not confuse good works with faith works. Good deeds and faith deeds are two different things and our eternal salvation depends on both of them.

The doctrine of salvation unquestionably teaches us that our eternal salvation from God's wrath requires us to be reconciled to God through the blood sacrifice of His Son Jesus, and then live a righteous, sinless, godly life in Jesus Christ by His indwelling Spirit. (See Romans 5:9–10; Galatians 2:20–21.)

It is all done by our faith working through love. (See Galatians 5:6.)

Let me tell you an example of the good works that God has pre-ordained for us. One week, our itinerary had us fly into Brazil on a Wednesday and further south to Argentina on Friday. As I mentioned, God rearranged this plan when the officer at the Brazil airport ordered us back on to the plane that was flying on to Buenos Aires. He said: "Pick up a visa there, then come back and you will be welcome to stay."

God's work unfolded when, with our new visas, we stepped into the busy airline office in the main plaza of Buenos Aires. We were hoping to get a flight back to Rio that evening. We waited quietly in the queue for a few minutes until out in the foyer we heard loud wailing and sobbing. I imagined this is what the widow of Nain would have sounded like as she followed her only son's funeral procession through the gates of that city, just at the time that Jesus was entering.

Being a stranger to Argentina I waited to see what would happen. Nothing happened except that the continuous moaning and sobbing of the woman grew louder and louder. Convinced that the six clerks behind the ticketing counter were deaf, and that the twenty or so people standing in the queues were immune to the screams of a woman, I turned to my wife and said: "Please go and find out what is going on in the foyer." A short time later my wife called to me: "Geoff, I cannot understand her—she is hysterical and speaks only a few words of English."

Leaving my place in line, I followed my wife to the distraught lady, who was now lying on the couch with tears streaming down her cheeks and deep sobs wracking her body. In Australia when I was a young boy during the Great Depression, I had seen my mother often helping ladies in a similar condition as they broke down under the strain of having a hungry family at home with nothing in the cupboard.

As I knelt beside the sobbing lady, I slowly pieced together her woes. She had come from Spain more than a year before to care for a sick relative. She had received a call from her own family in Spain that they needed her to return home immediately. Unfortunately her return ticket had expired and the airline said she was required to purchase a new ticket.

I left Margaret to console her and returned to the ticketing office. All eyes were on me. I went straight to the counter and asked to see the manager. He was a young man, likely in his early thirties. I entered his office and he politely motioned for me to be seated in a cane chair, which sat beside an impressive desk. I noticed that his door did little to reduce the noise of the moaning of the distraught lady in the outer foyer.

I said: "Do you know why that lady outside your office is crying?" He looked at me blankly, and did not reply. At first I wondered if he understood English, but then I thought I saw a tiny glimpse of compassion in his dark brown eyes. He appeared nervous and embarrassed.

I looked him straight in the eye and continued: "That lady has paid for a return ticket to Spain with your airline. But, because she waited for over twelve months to go home, you are demanding that she pay another fare. If that is the case, could you please tell me the amount in American dollars."

He replied in perfect English: "Yes, that is right, and her fare will be $800."

I told him I would pay half and asked if the airline would pay the other half, due to the special circumstances.

He replied: "We cannot do that."

I tried again. "Please phone your boss and see what he says." To my surprise, he called his boss, who reduced the fare to $700.

After discussing the situation with Margaret, we found that we would likely be able to pay the $700, and still have enough money left to get us home to Australia. It seemed like a good idea to both the Holy Spirit and us.

I handed him the money and as he lowered his head to write out the ticket, I noticed that tears were streaming down his face. He was still crying as I left his office with the ticket in my hand and his *thank you* in my ears.

While my wife presented the lady with her ticket I went back to the counter to arrange our flight back to Rio. To my amazement, every clerk behind the counter was unashamedly bawling his or her eyes out.

Nothing is impossible with God. He clearly uses members of His body to help the hurting. While we were only His big toe, he used us on that memorable day. I told everyone at the airport that we did it in the name of Jesus.

> I have fought a good fight, I have finished my course, I have kept the faith: Henceforth there is laid up for me a crown of righteousness, which the Lord, the righteous judge, shall give me at that day.
>
> —2 Timothy 4:7–8, kjv

Chapter 16

A Close Friend

For Christ is the end of the Mosaic law for righteousness to everyone that believeth. (See Romans 10:4.) Please note it is not the end of the law but the end as far as obtaining a righteous lifestyle from it is concerned. (See Galatians 2:21; 2 Corinthians 3:7.)

My wife and I have a secret friend. He is a reserved person, not talkative, but sensitive. His voice is gentle, yet has the unmistakable tone of authority. He is a happy person who likes to make his friends laugh. You will find him with people who do not put on airs and graces. He dislikes what he calls "skites" (loud-mouthed boasters).

We notice that he keeps away from rituals, does not join competitions, and seems to be very much at home with poor or humble people. Being generous himself, he has a soft spot for generous people.

He is not friendly towards the self-righteous or the pompous. He does not join conversations about money, prices, bargains, or possessions. He dislikes sinful talking and silly jesting.

He quickly withdraws from hypocrites and easily gets angry with them. You will not find him hanging around with those who are always criticizing or scoffing.

He delights in helping others and us when we have a real need. When we seek his advice, he is an excellent problem solver.

He takes us with him to visit the sick and lonely, and he is obviously very fond of little children. He is very forgiving and we have not yet seen him take revenge or disobey the laws of the land.

His main topic of conversation is Jesus. He is always telling others and us about how great our Savior is—but he does it in a nice way. He never gets pushy, but does not back down either.

He is friendly toward sinners, but if he finds that any of his Christian friends are sinning he will not associate with them, nor will he eat with them.

If he sees that people have preconceived ideas about how he should behave or if they try to control him in any way, he shuns them.

He loves to take us to meetings—sometimes half way around the world—where people worship and praise his champion, Jesus. He likes both noisy meetings and quiet meetings, just as long as people are joyful and ready to celebrate in the Savior's victory. He walks out of meetings if he sees insincerity, show-offs, forced or pretended holiness, rituals, greed, or manipulation.

When he meets uncritical and humble Christians, he has a very powerful effect on them. Some are overcome by the power of his love and kindness and they behave in strange ways. I have seen some shaking, jerking, running, crying, groaning, staggering like drunks, prophesying, seeing visions, praying in unknown languages, or laughing with joy. But, it does not embarrass him—unless they are pretending or showing off.

We too have learned not to take offense or to be critical of their behavior. He told me not to put God and His people into boxes of our own making.

He encourages us to talk to him and others about his champion, Jesus of Nazareth. In the company of our secret friend we always feel loved and loving. He is a wealth of wisdom and has a real insight into the things of God. He is profound yet simple. Nothing seems to be beyond his understanding and he can easily recognize evil spirits.

He stays away from doubters, scoffers, sinners, and worldly people. But, the ones that he absolutely refuses to talk to are religious hypocrites—clouds without water.

Our secret friend once said that God will never forgive anyone who tells our friend lies or who mistreats him.

If people invite our friend to stay in their house he will always say yes—but only if they believe in Jesus.

He likes to give us all sorts of gifts, both big and small, but will quickly pull us out if we look like we are entertaining temptation to sin.

He said: "If you return to sinning, I will part company with you."

Like us, he too knows how to cry, but if we get too down, he always tries to cheer us up and restore our peace and joy.

He said he wants to be our friend for life.

We would be lost without him.

My wife and I love him dearly.

His name is the *Holy Spirit.*

Chapter 17

Faith Through Love to Heaven

Can dead men sin? Are dead men under the law? Have we been crucified with Jesus or not? The Bible says that dead men are freed from sin. (See Romans 6:7.)

We could get the wrong idea that not all believers have enough faith granted them by God to believe Christ's promise that He sets us free from sinning, makes us dead to sin, and alive to God. (See John 8:34–36; Romans 6:11.)

Yet it follows that if we have enough faith to believe in Jesus as our Lord and Savior that we also have enough faith to believe that he whom the Son sets free is free indeed. It would not be fair to say that we trust a friend if we do not also trust his promises.

Not too long ago a man broke an English law if he failed to keep his promise to marry the girl wearing his engagement ring. Heavy fines were imposed for what was called "breach of promise." That English law applied throughout Australia up until the end of World War II.

Christ always keeps His promises. (See Hebrews 8:6; 2 Timothy 2:13.)

God says I will not suffer my faithfulness to fail. (See Psalm 89:33.)

Salvation takes place in our hearts and it comes as a result of hearing and understanding God's Word in our minds. When we put our God-given beliefs into action, it is what the Bible calls *faith*. As I believe, so I speak and do. (See 2 Corinthians 4:13.)

My dear friend Pastor Laurie Ramsay and I had the once-in-a-lifetime opportunity to see men literally moving a mountain in Australia.

The pilot of the small plane circled the area so that we could look down at the vast array of huge machines that were moving the mountain. Trucks then transported the gems down a carefully engineered network of roads to where the diamonds were to be separated from the earth. It was obvious that the task was going to take many years to complete.

Jesus said that mountains can be moved by faith, that our faith need only be tiny to see it happen. I'm not aware of anyone who has actually moved an actual mountain by faith, but millions have been reconciled to God by faith in the blood of Jesus Christ. Therefore you can be sure that if you have enough faith to have your past sins forgiven, then you also have enough faith to walk in all of God's promises in Christ.

The Bible is not talking about a "name it, claim it" sort of faith. It is talking about having a deep down, God-given, sacred conviction of the sincerity and truth of a promise of Christ. By speaking about our beliefs, they become the faith that brings the promise to life in His time.

The Bible says that faith is a demonstration of our God-given hope. Faith is the evidence of our hidden hope. (See Hebrews 11.) Faith is an action that requires results.

God created a universe out of nothing when, through Jesus Christ, He confessed His hope. His confession was the evidence of His belief. God thereby created the heavens and the earth. (See Genesis 1:1.) Please note that heaven and earth were not the evidence—it was the confessing that evidenced His hope.

> Beliefs are found in a man's heart, but faith is found on his lips.
> —Romans 10:10

The righteous walk in the Holy Spirit is from faith to faith. (See Romans 1:17.) We walk by faith in the great and precious promises so that we can be partakers of the divine nature. (See 2 Peter 1:4.) Every stride in the race to our inheritance must be made by faith.

The life I now live, I live by faith in the Son of God who loves me and gave His life for me. (See Galatians 2:20.)

Paul teaches that by walking in the Holy Spirit, the righteous wait in hope for their eternal inheritance that awaits the ones who live righteously by faith. (See Galatians 5:5.) The verse that I have explained is the Doctrine of Righteousness in a nutshell.

Through the Spirit, we wait for the hope of righteousness that comes by faith and not by the written laws of the Bible. Nothing avails but faith working through love. (See Galatians 5:4–6.)

When I am tempted to sin I instantly speak out loud my belief in God's promise. Those around me have heard me say, *Get out, I am dead to sin and alive to God in Christ Jesus.* The temptation immediately goes away like the morning mist. However, it must be said as a confession of faith after Romans 6:11 has become a deep-down inner conviction. Practice makes perfect!

If God's word verbalized is powerful enough to create a universe then surely it can easily overcome a temptation of the flesh, the world, or the devil.

I meet up often with well-intentioned Christians who verbalize their doubts. They do not believe in the entirety of God's Word when they say that they will not, and cannot, stop sinning until they die. They do not know they died with Christ in Baptism.

If they keep on this track they will be dead long before they die. Unknowingly, they are proclaiming Scriptures that describe the carnal man before being born of God. They are also denying Christ's victory. Christ's victory has not yet settled in their hearts. It can take time for the New Wine to become palatable.

While one who confesses to be a regular sinner might be very popular with men, that same person is an abomination in God's sight. "They profess that they know God; but in works they deny Him, being abominable and disobedient, and unto every good work reprobate" (Titus 1:16).

Speaking words of doubt can spread like a bush fire to the minds and hearts of those around us. God's Word says that we are blessed if we do not walk within earshot of the ungodly, nor hang around with sinners in our towns or in our churches. (See Psalm 1.) These days, it is possible to be confronted with the ungodly, the sinners, and the scoffers by switching on the television in our own living room. I treat words of doubt as spiritual poison, and I absolutely refuse to listen to them and I do not watch television for that reason, and anyway it does not interest me. I find it repugnant.

Paul teaches that in the end we will be presented holy, blameless, and irreproachable in God's sight if we continue in faith. (See Colossians 1:22–23.)

That faith includes confessing that *I* am dead and it is no longer *I* that lives but Christ who lives in me. If *I* am still reigning then *I* am under the law of sin, and racing along the wide road to destruction.

Righteousness means being blameless. Living anything less than a blameless life comes short of the standard required by God.

> But my righteousness shall be forever, and my salvation from generation to generation.
> —Isaiah 51:8, kjv

He took me like a grain of wheat to death so that He could impart to me resurrected life—a life of bearing good fruit and a life of righteousness.

I will be saved in the judgment because I have lived my Christian life without sin through my faith walk, which I found in the unwritten law of the Spirit of Life in Christ Jesus. (See Romans 8:1–2.)

You, Lord, meet with the one who rejoices and does works of righteousness. Those who persevere in *righteous works* shall be saved. (See Isaiah 64:5.)

Chapter 18

Lifestyles of Holiness

> *Let not the wise man glory in his wisdom neither let the mighty man glory in his might; let not the rich man glory in his riches; but let them glory in this: that they understand me, that I am the Lord who exercises three things in the earth: loving kindness, judgment and Righteousness…for in these three things I delight says the Lord.*
>
> —Jeremiah 9:23–24

It is our faith that releases in us the power of a righteous lifestyle. Michael Harper, a well-respected Christian teacher from England, writes in his book *Walk in the Spirit* that "brinksmanship" is a common attitude that robs us of what Christ longs to give us.[1]

We hover on the *brink* instead of confidently receiving. Doubts and fears assail us: "Will it work?" "How can it happen to me?" "What will others think?" "Will I be able to keep it up?" "Am I worthy?"

He concludes that if God has promised something, He cannot break His word. We should come humbly and honestly to claim our birthright. Anyone born of God cannot sin. We shall not be disappointed if we claim that promise, but if we doubt, James warns us: "That person must not suppose that He will receive anything of the Lord." (See James 1:8.)

Faith in Christ and His promises prevent us from being captivated by our own wishful thinking, which in turn leads us to acting presumptuously.

Thinking that our lifestyle will not be in question at the judgment is presumptuous. Presumption has always been the most common and fatal sin amongst God's people. The prime example is the behavioral pattern of the Israelites while in the wilderness. They disobeyed God, and then were amazed when His consuming fire devoured them—when the earth opened up and swallowed them.

Recently I went to court with a young man who was being charged for the traffic offense of speeding. He went in like a lion, but came out like a lamb. The judge used strong language to let him know that he was a potential killer and that one more offense would mean the loss of his license. Losing his license would also mean losing his job.

The young man was quickly and publicly made aware that disobeying the law of the land is serious business and carries punishment. He was speechless.

I wonder how many churchgoers will be shocked into reality on their judgment day. We are often convinced that we will be judged on *who* we are and not on *what* we have done. The boy who was fined for speeding was a member of a well-known and respected family, but that fact had no influence on the judge and his judgment.

Of course God expects that as Christians, we should always act righteously. When it's all said and done it is because of *who* we are that we are the first to be judged and indeed more severely. Jesus warned us that to whom much is given, much will be required. (See Luke 12:48.)

You may be thinking: "This book seems to be all about warnings." Yes you are right, and you will find that the Bible has the same emphasis. God's Word continually reminds Christians that only Jesus can keep us from falling. (See Jude 24.)

Jesus prophesied that "many will cry Lord, Lord" only to hear his words "I did not know you." (See Matthew 7:21–23.)

We will be judged by our lifestyle of works more than our words. (See 1 Peter 1:17.) Our works are the manifestation of our faith and our love.

The bride of Christ must be arrayed in righteousness. (See Revelation 19:8; Matthew 22:12–14.) Righteousness is about our actions, or our works. However, our righteousness is really God's righteousness working through us.

We are led again and again to 1 John 3:7, which cautions us not to be deceived, for it is the person who *does* righteously who is righteous. It is the Holy Spirit's pleasure to impart God's righteousness to our daily life. He keeps spotless our white robe that assures us of a seat at the marriage supper of the Lamb.

Let the skies pour down righteousness, let the earth open, let salvation and righteousness spring up together. (See Isaiah 45:8.)

The written Word of God points us to our Savior, but it cannot save us. (See John 5:39.) The living Word of God is our only Savior—His name is Jesus.

He is alive, powerful, and sharper than a double-edged scalpel. He pierces even to the dividing asunder of the soul and spirit, and of the joints and marrow. It is He who discerns the thoughts and intentions of our heart. All things are naked and open to his eyes. (See Hebrews 4:12–13.)

The New Testament describes Jesus our Lord as the second Adam. (See 1 Corinthians 15:45, 47.) We are in Him and like the first Adam, we start our walk in the Spirit in perfect harmony and fellowship with God. No past sin separates us from Him. (See Romans 3:25.)

If Adam had taken notice of God's warning he would have not become a castaway. We are also warned that nothing avails but faith working through love, and love starts with obedience. (See Galatians 5:6; John 14:15.)

The Bible warns us to avoid teachers that offer us freedom, but are still in bondage to sin and misuse the Scriptures to excuse themselves. (See 2 Peter 2:19.)

In 1 Corinthians 15:34, Paul says: "Awake to righteousness and sin not; for some have not the knowledge of God. I speak this to your shame."

Our Jesus is the great I Am. (See John 8:58.) He is the one who sent Moses to pharaoh, ruler of mighty Egypt. It took blood to set His people free from being destroyed by their Father God. In Egypt that fateful night, God's angel of death destroyed the first born in all homes without the blood. (See Exodus 12:12–13.)

This event took place to serve as an example for us that we are set free from God's wrath by the blood of Christ. The blood protected them from *God and not from pharaoh.*

The prophet Ezekiel tells us that God's people in Egypt had been living very sinful lives right up until the day of their deliverance. Except for the blood of the lamb as their protective covering, they too were candidates for God's punishment. (See Ezekiel 20:1–10; Exodus 12:21–30.)

The blood of Christ was not shed to protect us from Satan but from God. Jesus tells sinners to fear Him who has the power to send souls to hell. *We are not to fear our enemy the devil.* (See Matthew 10:28.)

Blessed is he who does righteousness at all times. (See Psalm 118:19.)

---

[1] Michael Harper, *Walk in the Spirit* (London: Hodder and Stoughton, 1968).

Chapter 19

Dreams, Visions, Deserts, and H. W. Connie

Hearken unto me, ye that know righteousness, the people in whose heart is my law; fear ye not the reproach of men, neither be ye afraid of their revilings.
—Isaiah 51:7, kjv

Those who walk in God's love no longer need to fear God's wrath because living in God's love stops all sinning. (See Galatians 5:15; Romans 13:10; Matthew 22:37–40.) There is no fear of punishment for the person that has been perfected through God's love and keeps God's Word. (See 1 John 2:5; Proverbs 10:12; 1 John 4:18.)

"Walk in God's love and give it away" are the words blazoned across a large banner strung along the balcony at the Toronto Airport Christian Fellowship. That banner shows that they have the intention of doing something with God's power through the tremendous outpouring of Holy Ghost love they are experiencing. Jesus says that it is our love for Him that causes us to obey Him. Walking in His love therefore keeps us righteous day by day. (See John 14:23–24.)

I have two roles in life: husband and father. If I were required to make a report on how much my dear wife and children love me, I would base it on their obedience to me. In God's kingdom, love and obedience are inseparable. It is the outpouring of God's love that has drawn millions from all over the world to this interdenominational church in Canada over the past eight years. What is God's purpose? It is to bring us into obedience to the words of Christ. (See John 15:10–12.)

We are obedient when we love others by giving God's love away. Would it not be wonderful to see that banner hanging in every church of the world and if every Christian put those words into action?

The words are scriptural and it sets the tone of the daily meetings at Toronto that are always attended by the Holy Spirit. My wife and I attended the meetings daily for one month. The meetings are low key so that any form of manipulation of the emotions is avoided. We kept going back to bask in the presence of God's love. I know of nothing better.

While attending the services, we experienced something I call a *fresh filling* in the Holy Spirit. I also experienced several visions and dreams.

On the mornings when our Jesus chooses to paint the eastern skies, He always does it differently. His first brushes of color show up very early in Toronto's mid-summer skies.

One special morning before dawn I awoke to see a bright vision in the darkness of the room. It was a snapshot of a large, official looking, brown envelope with the words *H.W. Connie* on it. There was no address. The vision lasted for about a minute.

While I did not understand the meaning, I knew it was from the Lord. When my wife awoke, I told her about the dream. I wanted her to be able to see the Lord in action when He chose to reveal the meaning of the dream.

That same night as we returned from meeting with the Holy Spirit, my wife started talking to a lady sitting beside her in the "church-hotel" shuttle bus.

The hotel decided to supply a church bus because of the large proportion of its guests going to and from the daily and nightly meetings. They were still talking as we took the elevator up to the third floor of the hotel. To our surprise her name was Connie, and her room was next door to ours. She had just arrived from Boston on the afternoon flight to seek the will of the Lord for her life at the church meetings.

The next day after the morning meeting at church, we invited Connie to have lunch with us and I explained the vision I had received. She also did not know what the initials *H. W.* meant.

However, the meaning was revealed to us during prayer. The Lord showed Connie that *H. W.* stood for *His Wife*. It was His answer to many weeks of Connie's prayers.

She had come to Toronto to seek His will concerning marriage. She had not expected to get a message via a couple of Aussies in a hotel room. God is faithful.

I have found that when we are under a heavy anointing of the Holy Spirit's love, He reveals many things to us in words of prophesy, dreams, and visions. It may sound strange but it is in line with the words of the prophet Joel. (See Joel 2:28.)

In using us, He left no doubt in Connie's mind that since we were perfect strangers from a far away land it had to be from Him and not from man.

Many people return again and again to Toronto eager to rest in the power and peace of His love. Who can sin when the anointing of love falls? No one. But when the anointing slightly lifts and we feel a little dry, it is then that we need faith in Christ and His promises to keep us free.

In this book I have attempted to remind us of God's plan to keep us free, even in the dry times, by a living faith in Christ and His promises.

In a dream I also had in Toronto, God showed me planes taking off at the airport. Each one had soccer ball-sized clouds attached in rows across the top surface of their wings. It was twilight and I could see that a fire within lit up each cloud. I believe that it was a picture of people returning to their churches across the world, carrying with them the special anointing of love that the Holy Spirit poured out at the Airport Christian Fellowship.

Later in the week I discovered that the fire was always inside of the cloud that God used to lead the children of Israel out of Egypt and to their inherited land. (See Exodus 14:24; Deuteronomy 5:22.)

Naturally, the fire was not seen during the bright sunny days in Arabia. Similarly the cloud was not noticeable at night because of the bright fire within. I respectfully suggest that since a cloud is vapor, it represents the Holy Spirit, while the fire shows His burning love for His people. Praise the Lord, for His love is like the coals of a fire that cannot be quenched by torrential rain or flood. (See Song of Solomon 8:7.)

Unfortunately, on their return home many had icy cold buckets of water, denouncing the validity of what they saw and experienced, doused over them and the spread of the move of the Spirit was often quenched by the opinions of those who had never been to Toronto. According to observations and reports that reached me, poisonous tongues inspired by fear and ignorance often put a stop to others catching the fire.

People often ask me: "Why would God choose Toronto to pour out such a special anointing?" I do not know. Why did God choose Jerusalem for His beloved city?

An honest study of the Bible shows that the Holy Spirit does not always do things according to man's ideas of decency and order. Just one example is when the Spirit caused people to behave in such an extreme manner that they were mistakenly called drunk. (See Acts 2:13–15.) Can you imagine the negative reactions when they heard about the event at the Temple Mount and at the feast of Pentecost?

Is it possible that our preconceived ideas of how we should act can be an excuse for shutting the windows of the church against the winds of change of the Spirit? We fear that our paperwork, our preconceived ideas, our plans, or our rituals may be blown away. We may even lose our image of our own dignity.

How do we react if someone is found on the floor of the church groaning for hours and unable to utter intelligent prayers? It is scriptural, but perhaps that is not the way we visualize the Spirit working. (See Romans 8:26–27.)

Are those that groan evidence of the fruit of the Spirit? (See Galatians 5:22–23.) We are encouraged to examine the fruit before judging the manifestations. (See Matthew 12:32–33.)

I believe that Jesus is saying that we must be careful to examine the fruit of the tree rather than judging the way the branches behave in the wind and rain. By doing this we will allow the Holy Spirit the freedom he requires to be able to reform and renew us in true righteousness.

I the LORD have called thee in righteousness…I am the LORD: That is my name: And my glory will I not give to another.

—ISAIAH 42:6, 8

Chapter 20

Doing Is Righteousness

Thus saith the LORD of hosts, hearken not unto the words of the prophets that prophesy unto you: they make you vain…they speak a vision of their own heart, and not out of the mouth of the LORD.
—Jeremiah 23:16, kjv

I have not sent these prophets, yet they ran: I have not spoken to them, yet they prophesied. But if they had stood in my counsel, and had caused my people to hear my words, then they should have turned them from their evil way, and from the evil of their doings.
—Jeremiah 23:21–22, kjv

Christian bookstores have an abundance of books written by pastors of very large churches that claim to be prophetic teachers. Yet, they often insist that our souls will be saved even though our lifestyle may be lost.

Standing before their congregations, pastors acknowledge that at least half either are, or will become divorced from their spouse. Many of their congregations are living in de facto relationships, some are homosexuals, some tax evaders, and others stir up strife or indulge in worldly pleasures. All of these are things God hates.

Yet these teachers teach and repeatedly write books insisting that it is normal for the saints to also be sinning. I believe that their consciences are gradually becoming seared. God calls out to us: "If you stand in my counsel and cause my people to hear my words, they will turn from the evil of their ways." (See Jeremiah 23:22.) But who is listening?

If we are not listening to God I can assure you that we are on the wide road to hell. Seventy-four chapters of the New

Testament epistles give me reason enough to heed their warnings, in addition to the witness from the Holy Spirit.

> Know ye not that the unrighteous shall not inherit the kingdom of God?
> —1 Corinthians 6:9, kjv

Be not deceived, Christians must do righteously to be righteous. (See 1 John 3:7.)

It is obvious from Scripture that now is the time that we must make a concerted effort to blow the whistle in order to halt the great falling away that is taking place before our eyes. It is, I feel, the falling away that precedes the coming of the Antichrist. (See 2 Thessalonians 2:3.) Even the media is lamenting the sad and sinful condition of the church.

Let my advice be acceptable: break off from sinning by doing righteousness. (See Daniel 4:27.)

Paul was writing about Spirit-filled, born-again, church-going Christians when he wrote: We apostles work so that, alive or dead, we might be accepted by Him. For all must appear before the judgment seat of Christ so that everyone can receive either good or evil for the things done in this life on earth. Knowing the terror of the Lord we therefore teach others. (See 2 Corinthians 5:9–11.)

Would you, dear reader, like to go out today and crucify the Jesus you call Lord? Strip Him in public and nail Him to a cross of wood in the main street of town? Put Him to open shame as a criminal? Kill Him? If you are anything like me it is too terrible to even imagine.

However, the New Testament says that if I am an established born-of-the-Spirit Christian that deliberately or repeatedly sins, then I am crucifying the Son of God all over again. (See Hebrews 6:6; 10:29.)

Jesus says, If you love me you will keep my commands. (See John 14:21.)

Paul, called by Jesus to be His apostle, was teaching Jesus' commands to the church when he wrote: do not keep company with any brother who is an abuser of mankind (homosexual), or a drunkard, or an extortioner, or who is living in a de facto relationship, or who is greedy for money and possessions (the latter are idolaters, and you will know them by listening to their conversations).

Paul then lays it on the line by adding: do not even sit down with them to eat a meal. (See 1 Corinthians 5:11–12; 6:9.)

But now I have written unto you not to keep company, if any man that is called a brother be a fornicator, or covetous, or an idolater, or a railer, or a drunkard, or an extortioner; with such one should not eat. For what have I to do to judge them also that are without? Do not ye judge them that are within? (See 1 Corinthians 5:9-12.)

Know ye not that the unrighteous shall not inherit the kingdom of God? Be not deceived: neither fornicators, nor idolaters, nor adulterers, nor effeminate, nor homosexuals, nor thieves, nor the covetous, nor drunkards, nor swindlers. (See 1 Corinthians 6:9.)

Therefore we are to treat public sinning by Christians as unacceptable and abominable; we are the body of Christ and Christ's ambassadors. Anyone who sins is of the devil. (See 1 John 3:8.)

Christians who are sinning in secret will be thrown out of the church on that day when the angels come to separate the tares from the wheat. (See Matthew 13:30.) We are not to go searching into the life of the brethren looking for specks. But when the speck is publicly displayed as a decaying apple, it is the responsibility of the whole body to remove the evil before it contaminates the rest of the congregation. (See 1 Corinthians 5:13.) The sinner must be given an opportunity to repent, but if no change takes place, we are permitted to take appropriate action.

Too readily we take the easy way out and under the pretense of love, we say nothing to those that are openly sinning. We pass our responsibility over to the Holy Spirit, but He will not relieve us of our scriptural responsibilities.

I had occasion recently to ask the Holy Spirit to show me the spiritual condition of a popular church. Fifteen minutes later I received a bright vision of a large sunflower with an ugly black spider sitting on the edge of the beautiful bloom.

It turned out that the sunflower was a picture of a fellowship that had been birthed in a wave of the Holy Spirit. Many spiritual gifts continued flowing. Like a large flower that attracts many unwary insects desiring sweet nectar, the church attracted many genuinely thirsty Christians.

It may shock you, but the spider turned out to be the *pastor* of that church. Like a spider, he was using the move of the Holy Spirit as a snare to attract the unwary victims he needed in order to satisfy his insatiable appetite for being in control. He had a spider-like spirit that needed to manipulate and devour the lives of men. It is a form of witchcraft that manifests as a controlling spirit. It is an evil spirit that is also adept at producing counterfeit spiritual gifts.

I now realize that God was showing me the entire history of His church. Every time He shakes us into renewal we quickly oust Him and start imposing our own doctrines and controls. The sunflower and the spider symbolize the church for the past two thousand years; God wants this pattern to stop.

It is fair to describe the history of our church as *man versus God* rather than *man obeys God*. Obeying produces a righteous lifestyle and proves our love for Him.

If we are walking in the Spirit, we will not be offended by what He is showing us in this book. We will take it to heart and draw back the curtain on the final *reformation* that will be based on His Doctrine of Righteousness. We will be eager to obey our great Shepherd Jesus Christ, the head of the church. We will have to drop our denominational pride and let Him build His house at His will.

This I pray: That you will be genuine and faultless until the day of Christ, and will be filled with the fruits of righteousness from Jesus Christ himself. (See Philippians 1:10–11.)

Therefore, put on the new man of God that God has created in righteousness and true holiness. (See Ephesians 4:24.)

Chapter 21

A Miracle in Ireland and Faith Has Works

*The L*ORD*… heareth the prayer of the righteous.*
—Proverbs 15:29, kjv

Along the beautiful and sometimes wild southern coastline of Ireland lies the fishing port and town of Arklow. One night when we needed a room, my wife found a pleasant looking home by the seaside that displayed a "Bed and Breakfast" sign.

Below us the giant swells of the Atlantic Ocean rolled in majestically as we signed the register. The young Irish lady had a sad far away look in her eye when she told us that her business was not doing well. In her quaint Irish brogue she quickly added, "Glory be to God."

I offered to pray for her and the business. She heartily agreed and emphasized it with another "Glory be to God." As soon as we laid hands on her and began to pray in the name of Jesus, she burst into tears. She was still crying as she showed us to our nicely furnished room where we could hear the muffled sound of waves breaking on the beach and cliffs.

Between the tears, she said, "God bless you," and left us alone. She had a kind husband who worked in the nearby town, and she had two children. We went to bed that night puzzled by all the tears that started after our prayer. Surely her business was not that bad.

Finishing our breakfast the next morning, I asked her to sit with us before we had to leave on our journey to Cork, a couple of hours driving to the west. As gently as I could, I asked her if she was feeling any better.

This time the tears came down steadily, but an amazing story followed. It turned out that she had been carrying a lifeless baby in her womb, but the instant we laid hands on her, it leaped within her and throughout the night was alive and kicking. Her tears were filled with joy and thanksgiving. It was our turn to shout "Glory be to God." A short time later we learned that she delivered a beautiful and healthy daughter.

God obviously answers the prayer of faith even when we do not know the need.

While we are on the subject of faith, let us have a brief look at some scriptures.

Paul states that nothing avails a Christian but faith working through love. (See Galatians 5:6.) So how does faith operate and how about love?

The Bible shows us that belief and faith are two separate things.

Our belief becomes faith by our words and actions. (See 2 Corinthians 4:13.) Paul's explanations of faith in Hebrews 11 shows us that there is first a believing heart and hope, which is followed by words or actions or both, giving legs to belief. James in his epistle states three times that faith without works is dead.

James gives us the example of how love without works profits no one (see James 2:15–16), and says that in the same way faith without works is dead. Sadly, many Christian teachers have misunderstood James and have wrongly taught that he was stating that faith without *good* works (love works) is dead. I encourage you to read it for yourself in James 2:15-26.

The writer of Hebrews also discusses this in the famous faith chapter, chapter 11. The truth is that faith has works of its own, while love has works of its own. Each has its own actions to bring it to life.

Faith may well produce good loving works, but it is a result of faith and not an integral part of faith. One example is that our belief that God would bless the lady at the Irish bed and breakfast became faith when we spoke it out in words of prayer. The result of our faith was an act of love by God. He did a work of love. Our works were simply the prayer of faith.

The prayer of faith in itself is not *good* works. Instead, good works as illustrated in the Bible are always works of love.

If we are ever going to make headway in faith and in love, it is necessary to understand the basic truth that love works (good works) are separate from faith works.

If you have already learned that "faith without *good* works is dead," then you have been led down the garden path. The Scripture says that faith without (its *own*) works is dead. (See James 2:17, 26.)

My dad often took my brother and me fishing when we were young. Dad and I fished while my brother read a book.

It seemed that dad and I were trying to see who could be the most patient. We would sit for hours holding our rods. We rarely disturbed our hopes by talking.

All three of us believed that we would catch fish, but only dad and I had faith. We were putting our belief and hope into action. We were doing faith works but my brother was not, and therefore he remained simply a believer.

Fishing was not *good* works, it was faith works. Sometimes on the way home we would give fish to a widowed mother of small children, which was doing good works, or *love works*. If we say that we love our next door neighbors, but never speak to them, then we are under a delusion and our thoughts of love profit nothing. Like faith, love without works is dead.

The reality of faith is found when we confess and live in Christ's promises. The reality of love is found when we live in God's works. The Doctrine of Righteousness is comprised of faith and love working together. When faith and love work together, we are guaranteed salvation from God's wrath at the judgment. (See Galatians 5:6.) Nothing avails but faith working through love. Paul also calls it "walking in the Spirit." (See Romans 8:2, 4.)

Paul tells us we need to meet together regularly to encourage our brothers and sisters to love and do good works in the Lord. (See Hebrews 10:24–25.) We are not asked to meet for the legal purpose of keeping the Sabbath; Christ is the end of the Mosaic Law for righteousness. (See Romans 10:4.)

For if righteousness come by the law, then Christ is dead in vain. (See Galatians 2:21.)

The righteous sin not. (See Ezekiel 3:31; 1 John 5:17.)

The lifeguards know it is impossible to save a person from drowning until they stop struggling to save themselves. It is the same with us when Jesus comes to save us. Until we stop attempting to save ourselves by using the law, He cannot help us. Nothing avails but faith working through love.

People will come to you saying "It is only the ceremonial parts of God's law to Moses that we need to discard in keeping us righteous," or "The Ten Commandments I will never forsake, for by them I am able to choose right from wrong." We naturally prefer the taste of the wine we were reared on over the new wine. Therefore, do not be surprised at what they say. I tell those people this Bible story: you will remember that Abraham had two sons. One son was from his wife's slave, Hagar, the other by his wife, Sarah.

One of the sons was born of the flesh out of an impatient carnal mind and he was called Ishmael. The son of his wife was born out of a promise from God by faith and he was called Isaac.

These two happenings took place to serve as an allegory for Christians that God would call two thousand years later. Hagar represented the coming covenant of the law given by God to Moses at Mount Sinai, which produced a people under slavery, just as Hagar was under slavery. After they reached the Promised Land, the city of Jerusalem replaced Sinai as the seat of the law covenant, and it has remained that way ever since.

Jerusalem and her children are still under bondage to the law and to sin. They are known as the Jews.

Sarah represented the new covenant whose children are free. We have a heavenly Jerusalem that is free and is the mother of us all.

As Christians, we are like Isaac. We are the children of God's promise. It is the same today as it was with Ishmael and Isaac. Carnal Christians who walk after the flesh and choose to be under the law of Moses continue to oppose those who are born-again of the Spirit of God (born by faith in the promise). Most churches today are divided into these two groups. (See Romans 8:4-6.)

The Scriptures say to cast away the slave girl and her children, for the son of the bond woman shall not receive the inheritance reserved for the son of the free woman. We have to decide to be either an Isaac or an Ishmael. Christ came to set us free. In Him we are all Isaac's—free children of joy and laughter.

> Stand fast therefore in the liberty wherewith Christ has set us free, and be not entangled again with the yoke of bondage.
> —GALATIANS 5:1

It is clear from the above Scripture that a person who looks to the law for righteousness and salvation will not receive the inheritance. This illustration that we have retold is in the new covenant Scriptures written by Paul the apostle of Christ to the little flock in Galatia (the country we now know as Turkey.) (See Galatians 4:22–31; 5:1.)

We are not to follow the presently popular way of looking to the earthly city of Jerusalem as our future home. We have the promise of a new heavenly Jerusalem on a new earth.

Even if you choose just one law for your righteousness you become responsible to all of the rest of the law and have as your future reward to be cast away like the son of Hagar. Paul says that if righteousness could come by the law, then Christ died in vain. (See Galatians 2:21; 3:10.)

For example, if you choose to think you need to keep the Sabbath in order to obtain your eternal salvation then you have cut yourself off from Christ's salvation and have fallen from grace. (See Galatians 5:4.)

A Christian is called to a righteous lifestyle by faith. We are complete in Him and are allowed nothing and nobody else. (See Colossians 2:10.) If we have a statue of a Buddha in our home or garden we are advertising a false God and a religion that is against Christ and the Holy Bible.

All sin is unrighteousness, and whoever is born of God sins

not. We are of God, and everyone outside of Christ is in wickedness. We are in Jesus Christ who is the true God and eternal life. (See 1 John 5:17–20.)

We are not boasting, for it's not we that live, but Christ, by His Spirit, living in us. It is He who keeps us righteous. (See Galatians 2:20–21.) Therefore there is no room for pride in the heart of a Christian that is walking a sinless lifestyle and no place for self-righteousness.

> The fruit of the righteous is a tree of life.
> —Proverbs 11:30, kjv

Chapter 22

A Tiny Flock

Enter ye in at the strait gate: for wide is the gate, and broad is the way, that leadeth to destruction, and many there be which go in thereat: Because strait is the gate, and narrow is the way, which leadeth unto life, and few there be that find it.
—Matthew 7:13–14, kjv

Many are called, only a few will travel with you on the road of righteousness. You can be sure that those who are blissfully hurtling down the road to destruction will be quick to tell you that you are on the wrong track.

The largest bank in Australia once coined a slogan: "Get with the strength." The bank's advertising agency was hoping to attract more business by playing on mankind's natural weakness to go with the flow. Follow the crowd.

In the righteous kingdom of Jesus Christ, we find ourselves in the company of the little flock. This little flock has pastures that are wide and green with many cool and refreshing wells. We give our first priority to seeking the kingdom of our great Shepherd Jesus Christ and His righteousness. We are a little flock that trots along in absolute obedience to the great Shepherd, for in Him we have perfect trust.

Everyday He leads us on the road of righteousness. We are His showcase. He knows that others will judge His worth by the condition and behavior of His little flock. If we stray from Him and the flock, He chastises us as gently as possible.

He also protects us from our enemies; we make it easier for Him by staying close to Him and each other. When droughts and dingoes surround us, He hand-feeds us while still in their presence. The baby lambs He carries gently and safely over the rugged patches.

We never fear any evil for He is always there with His crook, to save us from falling, and His staff, to fend off the enemies. He gently and safely carries the lambs in His strong arms through rough patches.

He gently leads those that are with child. When we are weak from old age or sickness, He picks us up and carries us on His broad shoulders. He has salve to heal our cuts and scratches and sweet fragrant soaps to anoint our heads and bodies when we need healing and peace.

He sees to it that we lack nothing that is good for us. Everyday we rejoice because we are in the care of His great goodness and mercy. At night He follows and guides us back to the safety of the walled sheepfold that His Father built. Before the sun sets, he tucks us in safe and sound.

Oh, praise the Lord for His everlasting loving-kindness. Even though we will one day enter into the valley of the shadow of death, we will not be afraid for He will take us safely through.

We have in these readings looked many times at the Scripture that says, "Nothing avails but faith working through love" (Gal. 5:6). It teaches us that the righteous lifestyle we need in order to receive no condemnation at our judgment depends on two basics: faith and love.

Faith comes by hearing the Word of God. Therefore we need to hear what the Bible says and walk in it. God's love comes to each of us from the Holy Spirit. Therefore we need to receive the Holy Spirit and walk in Him. (See Romans 10:17; 5:5.)

To walk in faith means that everyday we act on the promises of Christ which we already believe in our heart. My wife and I have a friend named Julie who always reminds us "God said it, I believe it, and that settles it."

We are not required to wait until we understand before we believe the promises of Christ. Faith is not about understanding. It is about believing our Father and stepping out in what He offers us even when we know it does not fit our logic.

For example, a wife may think: "If I obey my husband in everything, then logically I will become a zombie or a slave." But

I am confronted with the Scripture that says:

> Wives, submit yourselves unto your own husbands, as unto the Lord; for the husband is the head of the wife, even as Christ is the head of the church, and he is the saviour of the body.
>
> —Ephesians 5:22, kjv

This is followed as confirmation by the command to let wives be subject in *everything* to their own husbands just as the church is subject to Christ. (See Ephesians 5:24.) Logic will tell her, "If I obey that Scripture, I will finish up as a door mat." Faith says do it.

Jesus says that anyone who hears His word and fails to do it is like a house built on sand. When the flood comes it will be destroyed. (See Matthew 7:26–27.) The wife who is seeking righteousness will obey her husband, and the revelation of the wisdom of God's Word will follow, bringing peace and salvation to the home. Then, even when the flood comes, the marriage will still stand.

As men, we are often tempted to dodge paying taxes that we consider unfair or illogical. But we are met head on with the Scripture: the powers that be are ordained of God—for this reason pay your taxes for they are God's ministers. Render therefore to all their dues: taxes to whom taxes are due; fear to whom fear is due, honor to whom honor. Owe no man anything (meaning we must pay our bills on time). (See Romans 13: 5–8.)

If I am on a government pension, I am tempted to not disclose gifts of money or earnings that come my way. I reach out for all sorts of excuses, but the one who is seeking to obey God hears His voice saying *do it*. The Pensioner then experiences the peace that is the fruit of righteousness. Christ is the head of every man (male) and we must obey Him.

The above examples are given to illustrate what it means to walk in faith. It is what the apostle Paul declares to be at the heart of our eternal salvation: "For therein is the righteousness of God revealed from faith to faith. It is written the just (righteous) shall live by faith" (See Romans 1:17.) Obeying the Holy Spirit's law of life by faith will see us walking from faith to faith.

In today's moral climate it will not be easy to obey the following commands of our Lord Jesus: "Wives, submit yourselves unto your own husbands, as unto the Lord. For the husband is the head of the wife, even as Christ is the head of the Church. Therefore as the church is subject unto Christ, so let the wives be to their own husbands in every thing. Husbands, love your wives, even as Christ also loved the church, and gave himself [His life] for it…So ought men to love their wives as their own bodies. He that loveth his wife loveth himself" (See Ephesains 5:22–25; 28).

Now how about walking in love? Once again it is a matter of obeying the works of love. They come out of the Holy Spirit's love that He pours into our hearts when we keep our hearts open and expectant and soft. (See Romans 5:5.)

We will know that we are walking in His love and letting it overflow when we owe no man anything but love; he who loves his neighbor fulfills the Law. (See Romans 13:8.)

Love works are never against our neighbor. Therefore love cannot sin. This helps define the Scripture that says:

Love overcomes a multitude of sins; because "he that loveth another hath fulfilled the law" (Rom. 13:8). Proverbs 10:12 says "love covers a multitude of sins [all of them]."

Therefore, love prevents all sinning. Love without works is not love at all, and faith works without love works profits nothing. (See 1 Corinthians 13:3, 13.)

It was a sad day for mankind when the reformers of the sixteenth century introduced the teaching that love is not a factor that determines our eternal salvation on judgment day. Paul, however, consistently teaches that love in the life of a Christian is greater than faith. Recall again that nothing avails a Christian but faith working through love.

Jesus teaches us that on the day He comes back to judge us He will hand down His decision to you and to me according to whether or not we did works of love. His decision will declare where we will spend eternity and not our rank in heaven. (See Matthew 25:31–46.)

Do not be deceived; we are all appointed to stand before the judgment seat of Jesus Christ. (See Romans 14:10.) Peter the apostle confirms the teaching of Jesus on the judgment of a Christian—he shows that our Father in heaven does not discriminate unfairly according to whether or not we call Him Lord, but He judges us according to our works. (See 1 Peter 1:17.)

He is talking about works of love as Jesus was in Matthew 25, not about works of faith. You can read it for yourself in 1 Peter 1:17, 22, and Matthew 7:22. It is through our faith that we receive from Christ's Spirit the power to love others and to love God. We are first reconciled to God by faith alone. We can conclude that our eternal salvation depends on faith working through love. (See Galatians 5:6.)

I will judge everyone according to his or her ways says the Lord God. (See Ezekiel 18:30.)

And I will say to the righteous you shall surely live. (See Ezekiel 33:13.)

"The reason, therefore, why those who are in Christ Jesus are not condemned is that the law of the spirit of life in Christ Jesus has set you free from the law of sin…" (Rom. 8:1–2, The Jerusalem Bible).[1]

Confess It—Do It—And Live

---

[1] *The Jerusalem Bible*, popular edition (London: Darton, Longman, and Todd).

Chapter 23

The Beautiful Lady

Recently I experienced a Technicolor dream. I saw a city street filled with throngs of people scurrying home from work and shopping. Suddenly a tall building appeared on the left-hand side of that busy street. It was made of glass and was crystal clear.

My attention was drawn to a beautiful lady, gorgeously attired, gracefully mounting the internal staircase. Reaching the third floor she turned and walked to the front of one of the clear glass rooms and stood there like a fashion model. She had about her the regal presence of a queen.

To say that she attracted attention would be an understatement; she literally stopped traffic. I saw the cars banking up in a voluntary traffic jam. Drivers were jumping out of their cars to join a huge crowd of pedestrians who seemed to be transfixed by the magnificent lady standing alone as she looked out over them in a way that evoked awe. The people were still pointing up at her and gazing intently at her as I awakened from the dream.

I believe that the Holy Spirit was showing me a picture of His church after He has finished restoring her to His final glory. The lady was the virgin queen preparing to meet her Bridegroom King at the wedding reception to be held in the magnificent home of His Father. This church will attract the attention of the whole world for all are searching for the true beauty of love and genuine righteousness that they will see in her. (See Revelation 19:7.)

The Spirit of Elijah, who is also the Holy Spirit, has started making final preparations for Christ's bride so she will be ready and properly attired for the marriage feast of the Lamb. Are you accepting His work or are you hanging back trying to see if it is the work of the devil?

Do you not remember what religious people said the time that He first came to purchase His beloved bride with His shed blood? They said that He had a demon. There is, you must remember, no second chance if we miss our appointed time. Ask the Holy Spirit of Truth and He will discern it for you.

I have just returned from a reunion of seventy people in our district who acknowledge that the Holy Spirit, with whom Jesus baptized us over twenty-five years ago and who has continued His ongoing work in our lives, was and is the Spirit of Elijah. Without Him, we cannot be ready for that day when there is a shout from heaven calling us to the marriage supper of the faithful and expectant bride.

Let us rejoice and leap like calves coming out of their stalls, for the old man is crucified with Him. Our body in which sin lives was destroyed. We are no longer slaves to our old master called sin. We are no longer children of Adam.

We are now children of God—dead to sin but alive to God in Christ Jesus. The wage that God pays the sinner is death. Our gift is eternal life in Him. It is no longer I that lives but Christ who lives in me. Having been made free from sin and become servants of God we bear the fruit of holiness (righteousness) and our end is everlasting life. (See Romans 6:11, 22–23; Galatians 2:20; Romans 6:17–18.)

If we could achieve righteousness through any written law, then Christ died in vain. However, the righteousness of the law of Moses is fulfilled in those who walk not after the flesh, but after the Holy Spirit. To be carnally-minded is death; to be Spiritually-minded is life. (See Romans 8:4, 6.)

Without holiness no man will see God. (See Hebrews 12:14.)

And I, John, saw the Holy City (the new Jerusalem) coming down from God out of heaven, prepared as a bride adorned for her husband; and I heard a great voice out of heaven saying, "behold the pavilion of God is with men and He will dwell with them and they shall be his people, and God himself will be with them and be their God. And God shall wipe away all tears from their eyes; and there shall be no more death, neither sorrow, nor crying, neither shall there be any more pain for the former things are passed away" (Rev. 21:3–4, author's paraphrase).

VISUAL MATERIAL BY GEOFFREY HIGHAM

Four sixty-minute teachings are available on VHS cassettes or DVD. These powerful teachings, given to a live audience, complement the book, *Go and Sin No More*, and are ideal material for Bible study groups or sermons. They will help you walk in holiness and see God.

Please use the following address:

Geoffrey Higham Ministries
85 Mourilyan Road
Innisfail 4860, Australia
Phone (61) 7-40611326
Fax (61) 7-40614672
Email ghigham@dodo.com.au